Published by Moray Art Centre

Copyright © Moray Art Centre

2010, Moray Art Centre, Findhorn, Scotland, UK

Alison Wright: Reader, University College London, Essay and premise author and scholarly research
Hugo Chapman: Curator of Italian drawings from c. 1400 to c. 1800, in The Department of Prints and Drawings, The British Museum
Ernst Vegelin van Claerbergen: Head of The Courtauld Gallery
Aidan Weston-Lewis: Chief Curator, National Galleries of Scotland
Randy Klinger: Director, Moray Art Centre, Exhibition concept and graphic design
Freda Matassa: Curatorial Advisor
Scott Byrne: Exhibitions Officer

ISBN No:978-0-9565234-0-2

Sponsored by:

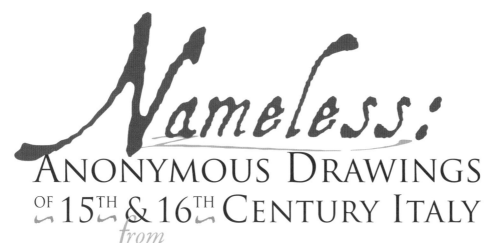

Nameless:
Anonymous Drawings
of 15th & 16th Century Italy
from
The British Museum
The Courtauld Gallery
National Galleries of Scotland

at MORAY Art Centre

Alison Wright

Contents

What's in a Name?
Randy Klinger

Fame offers remembrance eternal. Or does it? Of the great artists of the Renaissance, we have much evidence of their lives, artwork, colleagues, even their tax records. Historically, their fame and distinction have enshrined them through the generations by a name, but have these names actually reached us?

For instance, "Botticelli", *(actually, Alessandro di Mariano Filipepi)*; means "little barrel". The great painter, "Pollaiuolo" *(Antonio di Jacopo d'Antonio Benci)*, whose nick-name, *"Chicken-seller"* in English, ran one of the most versatile and prosperous studios in the Florence of the 1470's.

In an age of 'branding', our generation has become almost obsessed with celebrity and fame. Yet does name or brand necessarily guarantee quality?

Seventeen years ago, I started visiting what has now become to me a place of veneration. Walking up to the fourth floor, and presenting my blue pass-card, *(right)* and entering the Prints and Drawings Room of the British Museum, a space of polished dark-wood Victorian cabinets, an enormous glass ceiling, broad desks, and always the requisite white archival gloves. Yet, beside a curator or appraiser quietly studying a print or drawing, I was mostly there alone.

The British Museum, The Courtlauld Gallery and National Galleries of Scotland are stewards to some of the world's most exquisite collections; treasure-troves that members of the public can arrange to view and whose collections can be discovered on-line. Personally, the access to artists who lived 500 and 600 years ago has become a great source of inspiration and enlightenment to my work as an artist. During each visit to London, I always schedule time to study the drawings in the British Museum's seemingly endless collection. Each visit provides a close and direct encounter with artists who are, even now, great teachers.

It is well known that most paintings, fresco-cycles and sculptures of this period were joint efforts. The maestro provided the overall design, with the appropriate iconography and invention, and would carry out the most important and skilled areas of the work himself. A team of apprentices would complete the areas that required less skill, and in those genres in which they specialised such as drapery painting or landscape. In this exhibition, we have tried to make this experience accessible to the viewer in the adjoining gallery, in which an educational space allows the viewer to become a participant in the methods and, perhaps, thinking of the artists and their assistants.

But in drawings the artist is wholly present: it is as if they had never died and were sitting right beside you. Less refined than finished works, full of exploration and mistakes, with fragments of ideas coalescing and personal notes indicating what the final work is to become – drawings allow the student to study with the master. What a joy to overcome time and even death in this way!

In viewing these drawings one can magnify ones imagination in many directions. The Art Historian Ernst Gombrich wrote of the 'viewer's share' in completing a work; ones experience of 'filling-in' that which is undefined, hidden or left empty in an artist's work. In the Prints and Drawings Room, one can not only imagine deeply the life and hand of the artist, but one can hold (white gloves, please!) a piece of paper or parchment supported on the lap or on a table of a person who lived 600 years ago. This is an incredibly intimate experience: to be given access to an artist's private thoughts, feelings, perceptions and processes of synthesising ideas, their choices of restraint or expressiveness, and the whole raft of sensibilities that made them unique.

Each time I enter the Prints and Drawings Room, I feel a great sense of privilege. As an artist, I know the daily experience of aspiration, inspiration and frustration of work. But history exalts only named and praised artists to legendary status. We have focused in this exhibition, instead, on unknown artists. For over ten years, I would only look at the drawings of celebrated artists. Then, by accident, I ventured to the back of the museum's catalogue. What I found there is a treasure.

This exhibition is also about redemption; the redemption of artists whose names may well remain forever unknown. Who made them? Next to their 'superhuman' Renaissance contemporaries the artists seem to escape us. These small pieces of paper, beautifully crafted and preserved, offer us in the twenty-first century two opportunities: to revel in them as creations, and to honour a lifetime of devotion, nameless to history. Maybe what we learn from this exhibition, we can now expand to the appreciation of artists currently following their own devotion to, and pursuit of, beauty.

We wish to extend our very deepest gratitude and appreciation to The Trustees, Directors, Heads and Curators of Prints and Drawings of The British Museum, The Courtauld Gallery and The National Galleries of Scotland for making this exhibition possible and especially to Dr Alison Wright, who gave freely of her time, wealth of knowledge and her passion; our profound appreciation and gratitude. We give special appreciation to The Foyle Foundation, whose generous support made this exhibition and associated events possible.

Randy Klinger is the Founder & Director of Moray Art Centre

Life in the 'Anonymous' Box

Alison Wright

When the first, and last, exhibition to take the title 'Nameless' was held in London in 1921 it was designed as a vehicle for exhibiting the works of contemporary British artists under the aegis of the painter, critic and art historian Roger Fry. Initially hanging the pictures without reference to their makers, the stated aim of this anonymity was to 'dispel prejudices' when judging works from rival pictorial traditions. But for those already familiar with the artists, the affect would also have been to tease their powers of identification or attribution and try their knowledge – what is commonly referred to as connoisseurship.[1] Towards the end of the exhibition the contributors' names were finally unmasked to general satisfaction and, perhaps, occasional surprise. The display of early works of the Renaissance, as in the present exhibition, where all the names inscribed on the drawings are collectors' surmises, tends to provoke a flurry of attributions behind Print Room doors or in the press. But the current display neither expects nor invites such unmasking. Instead, the aim is to allow their anonymity to be, for the space of their exhibition at least, a virtue in itself. Identity, even authority – a word that suggests authorship is everything – does not depend only on a name but on the character, purposefulness and quality of what is being communicated. The drawings chosen here, made in an era when, with few exception, painters, sculptors and designers were unknown beyond their own cities, have been gathered precisely because they have distinct, varied and eloquent ways of speaking to present day viewers even in the absence of recognized authors.

Drawings, as objects that preserve the movements of a specific hand and with it, as Leonardo da Vinci put it, the 'movements of the mind', retain a kind of personality and intentionality that is quite distinctive to them as works of art. The pen or chalk is capable of inscribing an authorial presence as distinctly as a signature, but to look at drawings simply for that 'signature' can be to overlook or undervalue all the other forms of engagement drawings excite both through their own particular life and their witness to their age. With a name preceding the act of viewing we are predisposed to understand the drawings in a context that always-already delimits it. Such presuppositions are not always easy to quantify but might include an awareness of a broader artistic personality already rated as great or middle-ranking, dimly remembered anecdotes of an artist's life, or simply the comforting sense of the work having a known place within a set of other works by the same person (an oeuvre).

The appreciation of 'nameless' drawings is not a traditional feature of Renaissance scholarship. Indeed in an essay on the connoisseurship of drawings, the admired Print Room expert John Gere described an unattributed sheet as a work 'degraded to the level of an *objet trouvé*'.[2] The implications of the unattributed drawing as 'found object' are damning indeed: implicitly no longer a 'work' at all, the drawing becomes a thing picked up by chance, lacking any context and, therefore, the greater part of its meaning. While Gere concedes that unattributed drawings may still be beautiful and therefore give pleasure, the specificity of a place of origin, namely an artist's workshop and, with it, the possibility of a place within an artist's career is, for him, what offers the real satisfaction. It is true that assigning the pen and brush drawing of St. Sebastian, cat. no. 8, to the great Venetian painter Giovanni Bellini - a name first proposed in the 1920s but often questioned - gives it a more specific historical dimension and a new aura.[3] But the drawing of the naked youth, arrested poignantly between an ideal corporeal and spiritual state and unuttered mental suffering is powerful and telling even without this secure authorship. More importantly perhaps, dismissal of the nameless effectively denies works without attribution a place both in scholarship and in public view. The latter is a particular risk in an era, such as our own, that makes a fetish of celebrity, and in which the nameless is not only assumed unworthy of

[1] See Roger Fry's editorial in *The Burlington Magazine for Connoisseurs*, 38, no. 218, May 1921, p. 209 and Desmond McCarthy's review in the following issue, no. 219, June 1921, pp. 261-2. The exhibition, whose poster featured a diabolical modernist mask, was recently discussed by Samuel Elner at the Courtauld Institute Research Seminar: Modern and Contemporary on 12 January 2009.

exhibition but prejudged to be unpopular.
In fact drawings without attribution are far from free-floating 'found objects'; they bring with them not only a personality but a context of time and place. Indeed art historians may speak, in the case of the St. Sebastian drawing for example, of a work of the 'Venetian school, late 15th century', by drawing comparison with other drawings and cross-referencing to factors both internal and external to the drawing itself: the particular treatment of the subject, the handling of pictorial effects and similarities to surviving Venetian paintings. While the 'Venetian School' is neither a place nor an institution, this convenient art historical taxonomy (from *tassein*, to give order) has the distinct advantage of emphasizing regional differences in style and approach and not simply personal ones.

Anonymous, *Portrait drawing of a man,* 39.9 x 31.5 cm,
©The Trustees of the British Museum

The 'School' is a conventional pigeon-hole or label for a print room box containing unattributed drawings, but the idea that it is based on is historically revealing; namely that artists from different Italian, or other European cities adopted distinctive ways of drawing and making that are linked to their place of training and the priorities of their clientèle in those centers. Thus, for example, the practice of making highly finished portraits at bust length using black chalk, of the type of cat. no. 10 is entirely characteristic of the art of north eastern Italy, and especially Venice, from the later fifteenth-century onwards. The existence of many drawings in this category suggests both the cultivation of a distinctive regional skill and a specific expectation on the part of sitters who, on occasion, would be happy to have a drawn likeness rather than a more expensive and time-consuming painted one.

Anonymous, *St. Sebastian,* 18.6 x 5.8cm, ©The Trustees of the British Museum

In a world in which both the power to name and having a name are still ultimate assurances of recognition, as they were in the Renaissance, the place of the person or work without a name is always provisional, uncomfortable and awkward. There is no positive word to describe not having a name; anonymity is defined linguistically and therefore conceptually, only in terms of a lack. Importantly, beyond the point of their production, most of the various custodians of drawings, whether collectors, curators or dealers are personally, economically or institutionally invested in assigning authors to drawings. For a whole variety of reasons, curatorial, professional, popular and commercial, many art historians have continued to do the work of Renaissance writers on art, even while using an expanded set of critical and technical tools and different methodological assumptions.

The urge to attach personal names to works of art is a fundamental one in western culture; it stands at the very beginnings of art history in the fifteenth and sixteenth centuries and remains structural to the worlds of collecting, the art market and the gallery in the present. Finding a name is perhaps especially irresistible in the field of drawings where the paper seems to bear, misleadingly perhaps (see for example, cat. no. 15), such a direct, unmediated

[2] John A. Gere, 'Some Observations on the Practical Utility of Connoisseurship', in eds. Walter Strauss and Tracie Felker, *Drawings Defined*, New York 1987, p. 301.

[3] D. von Hadeln, *Venezianische Zeichnungen des Quattrocento*, Berlin 1925, plate 54 and pp. 38 and 48; see H. Tietze and E. Tietze-Conrat, *The Drawings of the Venetian Painters in the 15th and 16th Centuries*, New York 1944, no. 308, pp. 86-7 for skepticism as to this attribution.

5

and intimate trace of an individual mind. As John Berger puts it 'in front of a painting or a statue he [the spectator, assumed to be male] tends to identify himself with the subject, to interpret the images for their own sake; in front of a drawing he identifies himself with the artist, using the image to gain the conscious experience of seeing as though through the artist's own eyes.'[4] Whereas a great many Renaissance paintings and sculptures, even by painters or all-rounders as revered as Raphael or Leonardo, were produced over years and usually put together collaboratively in workshops, drawings of the same period are hardly ever a team effort. Objects produced to commission or acquired from workshops were generally designed to produce the *effect* of a single author (more justifiably assumed to be male than Berger's spectator), making any collaborators deliberately invisible. But drawings have the quality of authorship by default.
For this reason Renaissance drawings, though

virtually never named by their makers, for whom their value was provisional, have been - and are - frequently used to help construct and authenticate a body of work attached to a named artist. For the period addressed in this exhibition (c. 1400-1580), a period in which relatively few works of art were recorded in documents, drawings may be one of the few ways of accessing the appearance of lost or planned works and of rounding out the careers of artists by whom few works either survive or have been identified. The Florentine artist Giorgio Vasari, who in his *Lives of the Most Excellent Painters, Sculptors and Architects* (1550, expanded 1568) wrote what can be truly described as a first history of art, used drawings in just this way. In his life of the painter, sculptor and goldsmith Antonio del Pollaiuolo he refers to a design he owned for an equestrian statue showing the Duke of Milan 'the which design is in our Book in two forms'.[5] The two sheets, which he then goes on to describe (and which still survive, see illustration p. 7), bore testimony to a work that, for some reason, had never been carried through.[6] More importantly Vasari also saw drawings as testaments, or even memorials, to artists and to artistic achievement. His collection was therefore a close complement to his biographies of artists.[7] Drawings had to come with names. Thus he claims, unreliably as it turns out, to own drawings by the great Giotto, founder of modern Florentine painting, sheets that he describes reverently as 'relics' of the master's hand and superior to other contemporary drawings in his book. Some of his most prized possessions were evidently those drawings that were found in Florence after the death of his great hero Michelangelo and that he placed in his book where they testified to the 'greatness of his inborn talent'.[8]

Modern viewers might be surprised at how willing Vasari was to trim, shape and otherwise tidy up his drawing sheets, but such interventions were at one with his tendency to respond to single drawings as works of art. By providing elaborate mounts for single sheets and multiple drawings he gave the works a new aesthetic coherence. Most importantly for his new history of great painters, sculptors and architects, Vasari also grouped them in terms of stylistic handling or '*maniera*' and ascribed each page a name. This was far from a neutral act of

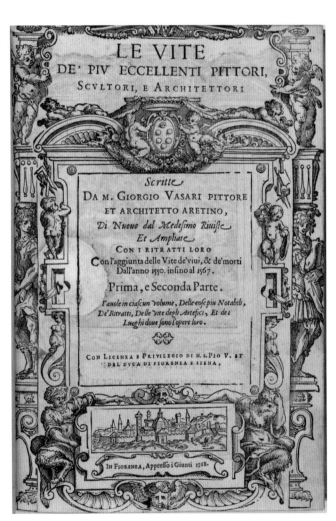

Giorgio Vasari, *Le Vite de' più eccellenti pittori, scultori, e architettori Vol.1*, Frontispiece
©The Trustees of the British Museum

[4] J. Berger, *Berger on Drawing*, Cork 2005, p. 4

[5] G. Vasari, *Le Vite dei più eccellenti pittori scultori ed architettori*, ed. G. Milanesi, III, Florence 1878, p. 297.

[6] Munich, Staatliche Graphische Sammlung, inv. no. 1908.168 and New York, Metropolitan Museum of Art, Robert Lehman Collection, inv. no. 1975.1.410, See A. Wright, *The Pollaiuolo Brothers: The Arts of Florence and Rome*, New Haven and London 2005, pp. 137- 42 and pp. 510-11.

[7] For Vasari's, now dispersed, collection of drawings see especially L. Ragghianti Collobi, *Il Libro de' Disegni del Vasari*, Florence 1974, 2 vols and C. Monbeig Goguel, 'Vasari's Attitude toward Collecting' in P. Jacks, *Vasari's Florence: Artists and Literati at the Medicean Court*, Cambridge 1998, pp.111-136.

[8] P. Barocchi and R. Ristori, *Il Carteggio di Michelangelo*, I, (Florence 1967), no. cclv p. 318 and IV (Florence 1979), nos. cmlvii and mlxii, pp. 90-1 and 238.

identification but gave order and assigned value in a way that allowed the collection to show how drawings were themselves worthy objects of attention or study. Good drawings were, like finished works of art, the acts of great men and revealed their innate talent (*ingegno*) even when they were preparatory to some more monumental work. In the present exhibition, the most spectacular example of a sixteenth-century mount given to a fifteenth-century drawing is that surrounding catalogue no. 4. The falcon devices and mottos in the lower corners reveal the identity of the early collector, the Florentine antiquarian Niccolo Gaddi who was Vasari's contemporary. But for Gaddi the mount also recognised the very complete character of the drawing, which is made on a durable vellum, as opposed to paper, support. By providing a richly ornamental paper frame with a (once empty) '*cartouche*' on the lower border, inviting an attribution, he gave the work the look of a devotional painting.

While Vasari is in great part responsible for the notion that understanding art involves assigning names, he has much to tell us about the ways in which drawings were used and valued in his times. Drawings and prints were, for him, the purest manifestations of good '*disegno*', a word that, at its

broadest, encompassed the whole purposive act of conceptualizing and carrying out a work (image, object or building), a work that would be both intrinsically beautiful and subject to rational analysis. Drawings indeed showed up good *disegno* in a way that paintings with their functional requirements and other contingent or subjective factors such as colour, could not. They were also means to ends and bore the marks of struggle, experimentation and, perhaps, failure. A number of early sources record Michelangelo having burned many of his drawings, sketches and large preparatory cartoons for paintings, perhaps to conceal the battle to achieve artistic perfection to which they testified.[8] By this measure, drawings were exposing. They might reveal an author, a trace of the self, but they could also reveal weaknesses of conception or vision. As the Florentine humanist Leon Battista Alberti argued already in his 1430s treatise *On Painting*, drawings and paintings should be made large so that any flaws would be brought to light and not concealed as they might be in a small-scale work where difficulties could be easily fudged.[9] Seen as responses to particular, recurrent artistic tasks and as a place of problem solving, drawings might ideally be preserved for many years in artists' workshops. Indeed, contrary to Michelangelo's introverted, protective attitude, drawings were more frequently seen as having collective value and they were preserved and exchanged by fellow artists to use as models, sometimes over generations. They were also themselves copied and, of course, used to make copies, close or free, of other artists' finished works, functioning as aides-memoire and in learning. I would argue that this was, in fact, the function of the sheet with a battle and a court scene cat. no. 3. The dependence upon a model with its own style and, in this case, apparently also imitating an earlier artist, obviously complicates the process of attributing the drawing considerably. Given that the ability to draw like another, older and more mature master was required at the earlier stages of Renaissance workshop training and could also be a marketable asset, it can also be misleading to connect the particular stylistic mannerisms of a drawing with the intrinsic personality of the draughtsman. The fascination of the northern Italian sheet with two naked men in combat, cat. no. 7, rests partly on the fact that both subject and

[9]Leon Battista Alberti, *On Painting*, transl. C. Grayson, ed. Oxford 1991, pp. 91-2.

Antonio Pollaiuolo, *Design for an equestrian statue*, Pen and brown ink with brown wash, background darkened with brown ink, 208 x 220 mm, Inv. Nr., 1908:168 Z, Staatliche Graphische Sammlung München

treatment deliberately ape that of another master, the aforementioned Pollaiuolo. The Florentine artist's work on battle themes in an antique style was probably known to the designer only at second hand through a copy drawing. Thus the choice of approach here came, to a large degree, with its specialised subject. The idea of the object of study being an important factor in considering how a drawing might point beyond its maker is raised in an acute way by portrait drawings, such as cat. no. 10, where signs of style may be suppressed in order better to 'reveal' the physical or psychological identity of their subject.

The *Adoration* drawing (cat. no. 4) referred to above bears a later identification in the right hand corner and repeated in the frame, attributing the work to the later fifteenth-century painter Domenico Ghirlandaio. This attribution is no longer sustained, and in fact relatively few of the attributions ascribed to Italian fourteenth- and fifteenth-century drawings by Vasari or his contemporaries have remained uncontested. It is striking that, because of the practice of mounting and the use of a paper support, Renaissance drawings frequently bear a whole archaeology of attributions and counter-attributions inscribed upon them by collectors and agents down the centuries. Over time, this naming process may have become more refined in some respects than Vasari's, and may even respond to new information, but it is more often based on, inevitably subjective, responses to visual 'evidence'. This evidence is hardly different in kind to that used by Vasari. Moreover, when addressing a period of widespread and often accomplished copying such as the Renaissance, attributions of more highly finished drawings like the *Adoration* can rarely be set in stone.

But drawings in the anonymous category have a further instability; they are potentially always in search of a name, awaiting some kind of settlement, promotion or relegation. They are a challenge or even an irritant to connoisseurship. In the process of organizing this exhibition one of the drawings, cat. no. 15 - a curious 'anamorphic' drawing showing a leaping hybrid horse driven on by a frenzied rider - found an attribution. The case has some typical features of the connoisseurial process, as well as some typical outcomes. As a category of drawing in a 'stretched' perspective there is little with which the mounted figure can be compared from this period, so in order to think about the possible purpose of the drawing the field had to be expanded to look at other drawings of similar subject, especially those associated with battle (cf cat. no. 3) or other equestrian heroics. It was in this comparative process that a number of works of similar subject emerged, one might even say leaped out, from the illustrated published catalogues of drawings collections, a remarkable resource not available to early connoisseurship. Not only were the subjects similar, but the distinctively brash and furious penmanship of the Courtauld Gallery drawing looked unavoidably comparable to several large-scale pen drawings by the Genoese sixteenth-century painter Luca Cambiaso. That this connection had not been made before probably relates to the anamorphic form, the self-disguise as it were, of the drawing: only when viewed from a radically oblique angle does the representation become properly legible and with it, the 'manner' if not necessarily the hand, of Cambiaso.

Visitors to this exhibition can choose to ignore the special viewpoint and, still more legitimately, the general attribution that is invited by it: the drawing

Detail of cat. no. 4, *Adoration of the Christ Child*, base of the paper mount©The Trustees of the British Museum

can remain 'nameless'. Nonetheless, once attributed, the drawing will doubtless have a different presence, even simply as a work whose identification other art historians may want to dispute. In Shakespeare's late Renaissance play, *Romeo and Juliet*, Juliet famously protests in her innocent frustration, 'that which we call a rose, by any other name would smell as sweet'. Why should Romeo be debarred her simply because he is a Montague, from an enemy clan? We might answer her that the rose by a different name might indeed smell sweet but, since given knowledge colours perception, it would not smell exactly the same. In a period and society in which both a family name and a good name (reputation) could be matters of life and death, the assignment of a name was enormously significant. It also signified, with rather less urgency, the authority of *cognoscenti* such as Giorgio Vasari. The ability to attribute is also an important sign of the authority of latterday collectors, curators and connoisseurs. But names are not essential to the enjoyment of drawings nor to the lessons they can teach us. Indeed it may sometimes produce a short circuit of comprehension, inhibiting the viewer's own judgement and closing further avenues of perception and thought. It is the contention of this exhibition that nameless drawings can smell, differently, sweet.

Alison Wright is Reader in Italian Art c. 1300-1550 in the Department of History of Art, University College London

Rejoicing in Anonymity

Hugo Chapman

'What sort of insects do you rejoice in, where YOU come from?'
the Gnat inquired.

'I don't REJOICE in insects at all,' Alice explained, 'because I'm rather afraid of them--at least the large kinds. But I can tell you the names of some of them.'

'Of course they answer to their names?' the Gnat remarked carelessly.

'I never knew them do it.'

'What's the use of their having names the Gnat said, 'if they won't answer to them?'

'No use to THEM,' said Alice; 'but it's useful to the people who name them, I suppose. If not, why do things have names at all?'

Lewis Carroll, "Through the Looking Glass"

Lewis Carroll's gentle mockery of the human desire to name things is an appropriate text to ponder for someone like myself whose professional life, firstly employed in an auction house cataloguing drawings for sale and then as a British Museum curator responsible for looking after the Italian drawings, has involved much time assigning names to pieces of paper. For the most part drawings were the working material of an artist and were rarely signed or inscribed since they were never intended to be seen by anyone beyond the maker and his immediate circle of assistants, a group whose daily familiarity with such works meant that there was no need for identifying marks. Just as we do not normally think to sign a shopping list or a reminder to our partner or housemates to feed the cat, so artists probably never considered that their studies towards a finished work of art would be pored over many centuries later, carefully stored in acid-free mounts and kept out of the light. While some would side with Carroll's Gnat and question the value of establishing the identity of an artist responsible for a drawing, I would argue authorship does matter. Stepping aside from works of art for a moment in favour of literature, in part because the waters are muddied by the monetary values attached to such attributions, one can imagine that if an hitherto unknown document came to light that showed that *Wuthering Heights* was actually written by Bramwell Brontë rather than his sister Emily, our admiration for the prose might not be altered but our sense of the novel's place in the development of English letters would require serious reexamination. The same is true of drawings, but the process of connoisseurship, the assembling of an argument in favour of an attribution through comparison with other drawings and finished works, is only valid if it can be explained step-by-step. The starting point for this procedure might well be an intuitive feeling, yet unless a clear case can be made to support that moment of inspiration it counts for nothing.

Authorship of a drawing is particularly pertinent because they are almost always the work of a single hand and mind, although there are exceptions such as the corrections made by Rembrandt to studies of posed nudes by his pupils. The individuality of drawings separates them from the often collaborative nature of the works that they frequently prepare, particularly in the Renaissance. Mastering the design process was a means by which painters, such as the Florentine Domenico Ghirlandaio in the 1480s, ensured that the output of the workshop was homogenous and of a uniformly high standard. Looking at the altarpiece or frescoed chapel by Ghirlandaio we are admiring a work designed by him, but probably largely executed by others following his drawings. A Renaissance patron was well aware that making art was a collective enterprise, in the same way that if we buy an article of clothing by a famous designer we want to believe that the price signals their personal involvement in its creative design, but we would not expect that the head of the atelier personally cut the material or sewed it together. The pupils and assistants in a Renaissance studio are for the most part as anonymous as the machinists who make the clothes we buy, and even when they are mentioned in a fifteenth-century document it is rare that we can actually identify their individual contribution. An awareness of the legion of nameless artists whose efforts went into the execution of large-scale projects, the majority of whom were schooled to work in the style of the master through a drawings-based workshop education, makes it clear why there are so many drawings that will forever remain anonymous. Such works are generally categorised by region – such as 'Florentine School' – or gathered under the name of a well-known artist, as in 'School of' or 'Follower of Leonardo'. The last-named category is the most amorphous because whereas School or Studio denotes that an artist might actually have learnt directly from an individual, to describe someone as a follower merely suggests that they looked at and were inspired by another's work.

The nuances of defining anonymity are perhaps best seen in the cataloguing of drawings in an auction house, an activity that can lead to legal action if it goes seriously awry. While it might be supposed that it would be much quicker if all Italian drawings that arrived for sale were catalogued as Leonardo, while Dutch ones automatically given to Rembrandt the established auction houses are in reality extraordinarily circumspect about proposing names because playing fast-and-loose with attributions would quickly undermine their reputation for scholarly reliability. During my ten-year stint as an Old Master Drawings auction cataloguer I learnt that it was often better not to advance a name for a drawing where there was uncertainty because in that way the buyer could imagine that he or she could have the triumph of naming it. With this knowledge in mind after my switch to being a museum curator, I have been known to point out that an anonymous drawing in a sale is in fact by an obscure artist. By doing so I am aware that an enticing mystery work will lose its allure and therefore perhaps be affordable to a cash-strapped institution like the British Museum.

As for the legions of anonymous drawings that I have under my care in the British Museum I do not feel (although perhaps I should) that they are an affront to my professional pride. The advent of the internet means that all of them are available to view, and I am delighted when someone emails me with a convincing case for a name to be attached to one of them. The moment when one moves a drawing from the anonymous to the named boxes has something of the pleasure felt when one triumphantly taps a piece in place in a fiendishly complex jigsaw puzzle. I know such triumphs are rare occurrences, and as my daily walks through the museum take me past countless artefacts whose creators will forever remain nameless I do not fret unduly. As the present exhibition highlights, a drawing does not require a name attached to it to be valued or admired: their intrinsic beauty and the beguiling intimacy of their creation remains undimmed.

Hugo Chapman is Curator of Italian drawings from c. 1400 to c. 1800, in The Department of Prints and Drawings, The British Museum

Ideals and Attributions

Essay by Ernst Vegelin van Claerbergen

Muirhead Bone, *Sir Robert Witt in his Library* © *The Samuel Courtauld Trust, The Courtauld Gallery, London*

In helping to establish the Courtauld Institute of Art and its Gallery, Samuel Courtauld (1876-1947) sought to influence the public understanding and enjoyment of art by training students who would go on to careers as academic art historians, lecturers, curators and museum directors. In 'teaching the teachers' he wanted to help ensure that the widest range of people would be able to benefit from the life-enhancing qualities of art and beauty, a notion to which he was profoundly committed. Citing the polymath Roger Fry as an example of an ideal lecturer, Courtauld stated, perhaps not quite accurately: 'he was not much interested in attributions, or in the local or scholastic sources of an artist's work; he drew attention to the broad human emotions and the inner spiritual content of a work and the artist's own aesthetic contribution and skill in expressing these.'

Samuel Courtauld was clearly not primarily concerned with a narrowly defined notion of academic art history. And yet when the Courtauld Institute opened in 1932 as the first specialist centre in the UK devoted to the study of the history of art, the most important challenge it faced was to elevate the status of a discipline that few regarded as a serious academic pursuit. At the time, and especially in the field of Renaissance studies, this inevitably involved the questions of attribution and authorship that Courtauld had instinctively shied away from: the essential groundwork of identifying the characteristics of individual artists' hands, ordering bodies of work and describing national and regional schools and periods. The challenges and needs were especially acute in drawings collections, with works often unsigned, surviving in large numbers and having been made for a wide range of purposes. Courtauld's fear, evidently, was that art history might detract from art appreciation, and that the name on the figurative label might disrupt the potential power of the individual's encounter with the work. Ultimately the risk was that art would remain the preserve of the wealthy and learned rather than 'be thrown open to all'. It seems that a preoccupation with attributions had social implications that were not in perfect harmony with the democratic role of art in modern society. Courtauld was not alone in expressing these anxieties, and they seemed to settle especially heavily on the study of drawings, so easily mischaracterised as the domain of an arcane closed process of connoisseurship practiced by a small band of privileged experts.

Notwithstanding these concerns, Courtauld understood the intimate quality of drawings and in his Presidential Address to the Association of Art Institutions in 1943 contrasted the experience of looking at a select group of drawings with the overwhelming aspects of visiting large museums: 'Many a private owner of a few drawings will gladly show them to a small appreciative group, and he will never be better pleased than when he can transmit a share of his enthusiasm to newcomers. Such an experience may very likely be more inspiring to young people than visits to public Galleries in the large regiments which one sometimes encountered before the war.' The Courtauld Gallery's collection of drawings is almost wholly the result of such enthusiasms, rooted in the inspirational unhurried encounter with the original work of art, but not disregarding the question of attribution.

The collection of 7000 drawings at the Courtauld Gallery is almost without exception the result of private philanthropy, having been shaped largely through a series of magnificent gifts and bequests. Rather than expressing an institutional collecting policy, it reflects the taste and concerns of a series of individuals, each of whom approached the idea of collecting with different criteria and purposes, and often with different means. The collection has its origins with Samuel Courtauld, who assembled an important group of nineteenth-century French drawings and watercolours alongside the great Impressionist and Post-Impressionist paintings for which the Gallery is now most famous. However, Samuel Courtauld was not a drawings collector per se and it was one of the Courtauld Institute's other co-founders, Sir Robert Witt (1856-1937), who established the drawings collection as an integral part of the Gallery, equal in every respect to the collection of paintings.

Robert Witt was only rarely able to acquire great individual works, and indeed this was not his primary interest. He sought rather to achieve a broad representation of the major national schools by acquiring works in quantity and depth, often by lesser-known or even nameless artists and, therefore, at relatively modest prices. The three anonymous drawings included in this exhibition are characteristic of Witt's approach. Acquired as noteworthy documents of the period, the absence of names did not deprive them of interest; Witt would have enjoyed them for their own sake and he understood that they would be of value to future generations of researchers in ways that he could not necessarily anticipate. As well as his collection of drawings and over 20,000 prints, Witt had also established a famous reference library of images of works of art. This had turned his home in Portman Square into a centre for art historians and consequently he was acutely aware of the forensic nature of some art historical research and the crucial role that drawings could play in this. When Witt died in 1952 he left over 3000 drawings to the Courtauld Gallery. Many of the artists whose work he collected have now emerged as significant individual artistic personalities but attribution was not his overriding concern. He set out to assemble an important study collection, the value of which lay not its exceptional individual aesthetic heights but in its context and depth and its ability to add to the rounded view of our understanding of the past.

Robert Witt's approach stands in sharp contrast with that of Count Antoine Seilern (1901-78). Seilern was one of the outstanding scholar collectors of the twentieth century. In addition to bequeathing to the Courtauld Gallery its very greatest Old Master paintings, Count Seilern was deeply interested in drawings. The collection of 350 drawings which he left to the Gallery is a true collection of masterpieces and includes examples by Michelangelo, Leonardo da Vinci, Dürer, Rembrandt, Rubens and Cézanne, amongst others. Count Seilern's great Renaissance drawings are the extreme opposite of the nameless works with which this exhibition concerns itself. All have been studied, published and illustrated in catalogues and articles. Singular masterpieces, such as Michelangelo's *The Dream*, enjoy an international fame rarely accorded to drawings and have been the focus of exhibitions and monographic publications. And yet even at these rarified heights identities are not always stable: an important group of drawings once attributed to Pieter Bruegel the Elder was transferred to the less exalted Roelandt Savery, and most recently new research has convincingly attributed a number of Rembrandt drawings from the Seilern bequest to one of the master's pupils. These drawings are no less eloquent witnesses to the past.

Sir John Witt (1907-82) followed in his father's footsteps by leaving his collection of British watercolours to the Courtauld Gallery and this part of the collection has developed into an area of special strength. Although the issue of attribution was perhaps less urgent and complex in this field than that of Old Master drawings, William and Mercie Spooner, who presented their collection of watercolours to the Gallery in 1967, delighted in the connoisseurship of the watercolour medium. 'Is it Con[stable] or Bon[ington]?'was a favourite prompt to consider the possibilities and pitfalls of naming. They wisely guarded against excessive optimism, 'the occupational disease of collectors and dealers', as their friend Leonard Duke put it. In 1974, a group of thirteen Turner watercolours assembled by Stephen Courtauld (1883-1967), Samuel's brother, was presented to the Gallery in his memory. The collection has continued to grow in this and other areas. Most recently, in 2007, the extraordinary bequest of Miss Dorothy Scharf (1942-2004) brought a further fifty British watercolours into the collection, including nine works by Turner, who is now represented by thirty sheets.

Each of the collectors mentioned above, and the many other individuals who have generously given groups of drawings or single works to the Courtauld Gallery

have engaged in their own way with their drawings, enjoying the immediacy of the marks left by the artist's hand on the paper, treasuring their beauty as aesthetic objects, delighting in the insights afforded into the creative process, and perhaps enjoying the challenge of research. These attractions have persisted as their drawings have made the transition from the private sphere to the public domain of the Courtauld Gallery and they co-exist happily with a wide spectrum of scholarly approaches and objectives, including the essential work of researching and identifying authorship.

The Dutch scientist and art-lover Christiaan Huygens recorded his visit with a group of connoisseurs to inspect drawings in the collection of Everhard Jabach in Paris in 1668: "[I] challenged the attribution of what he believed to be true Giulio Romanos and Raphaels, which drove him into a rage that made us all laugh, so much so that there would be hardly any comedy that would equal such a conference." Historical descriptions of groups of collectors or amateurs gathering to discuss the attribution of drawings survive from at least the seventeenth century. They suggest that the immediacy of the drawn or brushed mark on paper and the unique relationship into which it brings the viewer with the artist means that the question of identity is especially relevant or appropriate to this medium and can properly heighten the appreciation of drawing, rather than constitute a threat to it, as Samuel Courtauld may have feared.

The three anonymous drawings selected from the Courtauld Gallery for this exhibition have never previously been published or exhibited, and there is no record of anyone having sought to associate an artist's name with them. This superbly imaginative and timely exhibition asks what it is about these drawings that is 'nameless', why the absence of a name has caused them to be overlooked and what bearing their anonymity has on our ability to enjoy them. In addressing these questions it challenges more than just the anonymity of this particular selection of Renaissance drawings.

Ernst Vegelin van Claerbergen is the Head of The Courtauld Gallery, London

[1] Anna Tummers, 'By His Hand': The Paradox of Seventeenth-Century Connoisseurship' in A. Tummers and K. Jonckheere eds., Art Market and Connoisseurship, Amsterdam, 2008

Catalogue of Drawings

1. The Virgin Mary and two Holy Women

British Museum 1909,0109.1, Popham and Pouncey cat. no. 282
Metalpoint with white highlighting, largely oxidized, on lilac prepared paper (patched at top left).
16.2 cm x 12.5 cm

Select bibliography: *Catalogue of Drawings exhibited...Messrs. Obach*, Nov/Dec 1908, no, 29; Suida, 1909/10, I, no. 1; British Museum *Guide*, 1912, no.1; Stix and Fröhlich-Bum, 1926, p. 1, under cat. no. 1; Popham and Pouncey, 1950, I, pp. 179-180; Magagnato, 1958, p.51; Ragghianti, 1987, p. 113, fig. 220; Birke and Kertész, 1997, IV, under 24022, p. 2308; Karet, 2002, p.155, illustrated p. 154

When this drawing was made, probably in the early fifteenth century, it would have been the huddle of three holy women that would have been quickly recognizable, rather than the hand of the artist. Together the mourners appeared at the foot of the cross in expanded narrative depictions of Christ's Crucifixion. At the centre the Virgin Mary, falling to one side, still dominates the composition by her stature. She is buttressed by two sainted women, sometimes identified with two other Marys mentioned in the Gospels as followers of Christ. As a trio they form a motif of compassion, intended to show the 'co-suffering' of the Virgin with her son, a theme that itself became a rich subject for devotion by the later Middle Ages.[1] Mary, as mother of the Crucified Christ, is so wracked with anguish that she faints in a kind of death-like sympathy with him. The flanking women, meanwhile, present another example of sympathetic feeling by attempting to sustain her. In this drawing, the appeal to the devout viewer's own fellow feeling is emphasized by the expression of sorrow that the left hand woman turns towards us, with somewhat neckless discomfort. Her lament is echoed back by the woman in profile, demonstrating their pious assumption of the Virgin's pain. The group is highly orchestrated in formal terms, too. The three ovoid heads, backed by extended haloes, are tucked in next to one another at a variety of angles above the larger unifying oval described by their heavily draped and elongated bodies. A pair of drooping hands is aligned centrally in an arrangement of mimetic lifelessness. The figures appear welded together by a continuous curtain of drapery, so that the three bodies may be read in terms of the sweeping and controlled play of looping or cascading folds. Though the upper bodies and arms give a diagonal emphasis, the effect remains stable, even graceful. These same visual characteristics serve thematically to suggest heavy weeping so that the whole becomes a kind of meditation on grief. Seen in these terms, the group provides a visual equivalent to the famously emotive 'Lamentation of the Blessed Virgin', a medieval devotional poem in which the Virgin gives instruction on the heartfelt sorrow appropriate to Christ's suffering.

The drawing is executed with the softness and precision of metalpoint – a stylus that leaves an indelible line only on specially prepared paper – producing a suitably mournful combination of subtle greys against a lilac ground. White highlighting, which has mostly oxidized to black, would originally have offered a stronger sense of projection, but its faded pallor is retained only around the central hands. Neither the origins nor date of this drawing have proved easy to pinpoint. Though the pattern-making in the borders of the drapery is a typical late Gothic effect, and the fashion in the head gear of the right hand figure would also suggest a date in the late fourteenth or early fifteenth century, the distinctive oval forms in the drapery over the shoulders, or where it presses against the lower legs, is hard to match in any of the regions to which this drawing has been related – Umbria or the Marches, the north east of Italy and more recently Lombardy.[2] Curiously a pen and ink drawing of the same group - more spatially ambitious but without the same decorative logic – survives in Vienna. But as that hesitant drawing is surely not an 'original' invention either, it leaves the status of the British Museum sheet just as uncertain. Perhaps both are copies, in very different spirits, of a lost model.

[1] See especially for the textual and dramatic traditions of the Virgin's compassion developed from 1100 onwards *T.H Bestul, Texts of the Passion: Latin Devotional Literature and Medieval Society*, Philadelphia 1996, (Chap. 4 and Appendix 1 for the St. Bernard's famous 'Lamentation of the Blessed Virgin') and S. Sticca, *The Planctus Mariae in the Dramatic Tradition of the Middle Ages*, transl. Athens and London 1988

[2] The latter suggestion, by Andrea de' Marchi, is unpublished.

[3] It has been plausibly connected by Karet (2002) with a Veronese painter, Giovanni Badile of the first half of the fifteenth century.

17

2. Group of six figures in devotional poses
Verso: [The lower half of a seated, draped figure]

British Museum 1860,0616.52, Popham and Pouncey cat. no. 271
Pen and brown ink on cream paper.
14.9 x 17 cm

Select bibliography: Ottley,1823, p. 8; Berenson, 1938, II, no. 2756A, p. 353; Popham and Pouncey, 1950, I, pp. 171-2; Grassi, 1956, p. 60; Grassi, 1961, no. 4, p. 127; Degenhart and Schmitt, 1968, I-2, no. 193, I-4, pl. 215a-b; Wood, 2003, p. 111, fig. 7.29.

This lively double row of elegant figures in attitudes of devotion was, like cat. no. 1, another set piece for religious painters of the late fourteenth or early fifteenth century. Even with the object of their gaze missing from the sheet, it is obvious from the postures of prayer, humility and self-dedication (hands crossed or held to the breast) that they stand in the presence of the sacred. Ordered files of overlapping figures like these, studies of variety within uniformity, are most common in paintings of the heavenly court and especially in depictions of the Coronation of the Virgin, which was usually shown taking place in the presence of the saints in heaven. Though the figure to the far right apparently holds a palm of martyrdom before her right shoulder, none of the attendants have haloes. Unless these have been omitted by chance, it seems more likely that we are looking at a selection of the Christian Blessed, saved souls who are enjoying a vision of the godhead at the end of time. In the early nineteenth-century (when the sheet had already been in England for two hundred years), William Young Ottley optimistically ascribed this drawing to the great Florentine narrative painter Giotto and it may be that he had in mind the famous Last Judgement fresco painted by Giotto in Padua. In this, the Elect from all walks of life are arrayed in grateful reverence at the right hand of Christ. While our drawing is certainly later than this – perhaps by as much as a century to judge by the drapery style with its beautiful, looping folds - it is typical of Giotto's tradition and of Florentine painting in general. This tradition is revealed above all in a keen sense for the bodily volume of figures, brought to form by the use of consistent pen shading so that they appear illuminated from a single source. Interestingly here, that light source is not from the right - as we might expect given the subject - but from above and behind so that the figures gain in relief while their faces are underplayed. The handling of the pen, like the figures it describes, is notably controlled; it is also confident, reminiscent in this respect of the rapid, simplified underdrawings called *sinopie* that underlay Florentine fresco paintings in the late medieval period and early Renaissance. The draughtsman, practiced from a young age in the use of pen and ink, which does not allow for changes of mind, knows his medium and how to manipulate it. The ink has been allowed to pool for the darkest accents or, with the quill tilted to its narrowest, produce long parallel lines that fade into the areas of highlight. The most finished figures are those in the foreground while others, subsequently added in behind, are in varying stages of completion. But there was clearly no need to take them further. The straightforward composition offers few difficulties and it is likely that, subsequent to this rapid group essay, the artist would have gone on to more detailed studies of areas like the heads, which present more complex problems. The anonymity of this drawing sits fittingly with that of the Blessed. While clearly retaining their social identities they are now beyond individuality, reduced to type: two older women with veiled heads, younger girls behind with loose hair uncovered, one with a diadem, and to the rear a crop-headed figure, with jauntier drapery - surely a nobleman rather than another woman as is usually assumed. The devotional gaze, that reduces these holy attendants to profiles, points beyond itself and was intended as an invitation for a painting's beholders to follow suit by turning their eyes and minds to God. In this small drawing we are left to gaze, with a quite different intentness, at these heavenly courtiers who find their fulfillment in a state of eternal looking on.

19

3. Battle Scene, probably representing the battle between Romans and the troops of Emperor Barbarossa before Rome
Verso: Scene of supplication, probably Otto interceding for peace with Venice before his father, the Emperor Barbarossa

British Museum SL,5226.57, Popham and Pouncey cat. no. 299
Pen and brown ink over traces of black chalk on paper tinted pink from the recto.
Watermark of a pair of pincers
27.1 x 18.3 cm

Inscribed at bottom edge of recto in 16th-century Flemish or German hand 'Hüpsh Merte' perhaps for 'Hübsch Martin' (Martin Schongauer, a 15th-century German artist)

Select bibliography: Colvin,1884(1) p. 338 ff. and 1884(2), p. 282; Müntz, 1897, pp. 69-72; Hill, 1905, pp. 32, 33-34, 241; van Marle, VIII, 1927, pp. 68-70, 72 and fig. 38, Pudelko, 1934, pp. 254 and 256-7, fig. 22; Degenhart, 1945, pp. 26, 27, 51 and 71 f and 51 figs. 23 and 22; Popham, 1945, p. 130; Popham and Pouncey, 1950, no. 299, pp. 189-90; Mellini, 1965, p. 80; Pignatti, 1971, pp. 91-217; Paccagnini,1973, p.138, p. 161; Degenhart and Schmitt, 1980, II-1, pp. 117-24 and II-3, cats. 647-649; Wolters, 1983, 168-9; Fortini Brown, 1988, p. 41 Catalogue IV.2; Humfrey, 1989, p. 301 and p. 336 note 16, p. 335, note 5; De Marchi, 1992, p. 64, p. 94 n. 123 and p. 95 n. 151; Cordellier et al, 1996, esp. cat. no. 3, pp. 35-40; Skerl Del Conte, 1998, pp. 47-71 at pp. 47-52; Richards 2000, pp. 41-2.

The lively study of chivalric combat on the recto of this sheet is surprisingly neatly drawn for a battle scene. Despite the multitude and difficulty of the figures, there are hardly any corrections in the pen lines, which follow a barely visible underdrawing. This strongly suggests the draughtsman was following an existing composition with care, probably a painting, rather than working in an exploratory way from scratch. What he records is not only the complexity of the horse and rider groups but also something of a painting's tonal values with the various groups standing out in relief against a darker ground. Only to the lower right has the drawing faded. What survives on this slightly trimmed sheet are four clear groups that demonstrate how even a battle can submit to an intelligent compositional logic. The first - along the top edge, but seen slightly from above - is a head- to-head clash of ranked horsemen wielding lances. They are led from the left by a helmeted figure with an eagle crest bearing a sword and riding a caparisoned charger. At the centre, a looser grouping of slightly larger horsemen features a prancing lancer who has overcome a fallen knight, while another leaps away from the viewer. These three establish the spatial dynamics of the central field through a series of viewpoints that produce an effect of depth. The two smaller groups in close combat to the bottom left and right include foot soldiers seen in bird's-eye view. The overall effect of these groupings is to draw the eye around the battlefield following the varieties of visual interest, without producing a strict sense of continuous space or a compositional centre. The army from the left appears to have brought the fight to the enemy camp under the aegis of the eagle, symbol of the Holy Roman Empire. The careering rider by the upper tent, whose horse has collapsed, and the dramatically contorted knight who falls backwards towards the viewer, look like augurs of the encampment's defeat. With a flexible pen line, the draughtsman admiringly records the lunging, hacking and tumbling poses and the foreshortened and beautiful curves of the great-necked warhorses.

The pictorial challenge of the composition on the reverse of the sheet is altogether different, representing both a strongly centralized spatial and social order. Here the draughtsman records just one half of a symmetrical architectural structure, saving time since the right half would mirror what is already drawn. Taking place beneath its Gothic framing arches is a court scene with a ritual of submission and audience. The elaborate sculptural decoration of the skyline (so like those used by the painter Pisanello in the Veronese Brenzoni monument, 1426) recalls that of the medieval palace of the Doge in Venice. But the repeated motif of the imperial eagle in the finials sets the story in a different time and place. The centralized perspective construction of the pavement and parapets of the foreground explicitly accommodate the viewer as if, like the reverencing courtiers who have bared their heads, he or she is a participant in the ritual approach to the enthroned emperor. The

Recto

ruler raises his left hand in a gesture of speech or acknowledgement while, to the right, a cowled cleric turns back towards two knights, one holding a falcon. Playfully undermining the solemnity of the scene, while fully underwriting its chivalric message, a trio of dogs (symbols of faithfulness) tease one another in the foreground.

For an anonymous drawing, this a very well known and frequently cited work – if one that has been scarcely analysed. Such exposure has more to do with what the double-sided sheet depicts than with who made it, though these two questions are not fully separable. Although there is no consensus as to who authored the original scenes of battle and audience that are shown on either side of the sheet, it is generally agreed that these drawings are made after two of the famous stories of the life of the twelfth-century Doge of Venice Alexander III – shown in some 22 fields – that were painted in the Hall of the Great Council in the Doge's Palace in Venice. Their subjects, recorded before their destruction by fire in the late fifteenth century, included the Battle between the troops of the Holy Roman Emperor Frederick Barbarossa and the Romans by Porta S. Angelo, and Otto, son of Barbarossa, interceding for peace with Venice before his father. The lost murals were painted in two periods, the first in the 1360s, after which the scenes were badly damaged by fire, and the second from 1409. This second campaign, undertaken by the young Pisanello (now best known for his surviving battle scenes in Mantua) and another great narrative painter Gentile da Fabriano, was largely one of restoration and completion. It has been argued that the costumes worn by the figures in combat and at court belong to the earlier period, though in fact the pointed helmets were worn into the early fifteenth century and the helmets with sweeping neck defenses are not, presently, known before 1410.[1] Certainly the complexity of the poses assumed by both horses and figures is far more sophisticated than even the most ambitious late Trecento murals, such as those of the Veronese painter Altichiero. I would argue (along with van Marle, Degenhart, Paccagnini and Pignatti) that the scenes copied by the draughtsman, perhaps in the early to mid 1400s, represent the post 1409 re-working of the damaged scenes that had first been executed by Guariento and his workshop.[2] In this reworking, the brilliant young Pisanello adopts only in part the fashions of the revered works he was asked to restore and complete, and took the opportunity to display his unmatched understanding of the drama of the foreshortened figure. When the Paduan doctor Michele Savonarola of Padua, writing in the 1440s, saw the still intact paintings in Venice he recorded that the "appearance of the figures and the representations of so many painted battles are so much admired, that no one wishes to leave". Our draughtsman was surely among these captivated admirers. It is perhaps not fanciful to imagine him seated with paper in hand before the murals, ensuring that he would remember and learn from what he had seen. The survival of this impressive, if self-effacing, sheet allows us to do the same.

[1] I am most grateful to Dirk Breiding, Assistant Curator in the Department of Arms and Armor at the Metropolitan Museum of Art, New York, for his advice on the dating of the military dress.

[2] Colvin and Fortini Brown prefer the period 1376-68. Cordellier, Fortini Brown and De Marchi all note the difference in scale relationships and treatment of space to late Trecento painting. Cordellier favours a later artist, but does not think this can be the picture that Bartolommeo Fazio admired by Pisanello in the Hall of the Great Councul, since this is described as including smiling children as well as a grimacing priest. as a grimacing priest.

Verso

23

4. Adoration of the Christ Child

British Museum 1860,0619.49, Popham and
Pouncey cat. no. 279
Pen and brown ink and brown wash, with
discoloured white highlighting of rays of light,
on vellum
29.7 x 22 cm (area of vellum), 46. x 37.4 cm
(including paper mount).

Inscribed: "Domen.co Ghirlandajo" and on mount:
"DOMEN.CO GHIRLAN/DAIO" in a (19th-
century?) hand. On the mount, the italianised
French motto"TANCHE GIE VIV[R]AI"

Select bibliography: Metz, 1798 (expanded edition
of 1789); Berenson, 1938, II, no. 2508, p. 328;
Wickhoff, 1899, p. 213; van Marle, XI, 1929, p. 396
and fig. 245; Pudelko 1934(2), p. 200; Popham and
Pouncey, 1950, I, pp. 178-9 and p. 209; Degenhart
and Schmitt, I, 2, p. 557; Sutton,1985, p. 136, fig. 1.

This large fifteenth-century composition was evidently
still valued by the later eighteenth century when,
attributed to the great Florentine painter Fra Filippo
Lippi, it was engraved by Conrad Metz. Tellingly, the
engraving included the decorative paper mount,
probably that of the sixteenth-century Florentine
collector Niccolò Gaddi, which treats the drawing as a
complete picture in its own right.[1] The fact that the
drawing was made on vellum, a smooth, expensive
type of hide from a young animal (usually a calf)
suggests that it was designed from the outset to be
treasured and preserved. Although the drawing could
easily have been used as the basis of a devotional print,
there is no reason to assume it was made in
preparation for a painting. Indeed it seems more
plausible that this was an exercise in 'devotional
drawing' by a *maestro di disegno* or expert in drawing
and design for whom drawing was a form of picture-
making. This draughtsman, who apparently knew the
much-admired small altarpieces by Fra Filippo Lippi
(illustrated, c. 1459) in which the Virgin is shown
kneeling in reverence before her Child, has picked up
on the popularity of the subject in Florence in order
to make his quite original variant.[2] Dating, I would
argue, to the 1460s, the sheet belongs in a similar
category to the selectively painted pen and wash
drawing on parchment of the *Adoration of the
Shepherds* by the Florentine Pesellino now in the

Louvre.[3] In the British Museum composition, St.
Joseph is consigned to the middleground where he
leans on his staff beside the thatched stable. At the
same time the boy St. John the Baptist, unnoticed by
the holy family (and by any earlier accounts of this
drawing), is approaching out of the wilderness,
signaled by an avenue of tall trees receding to the left.
What he will encounter is a scene of exceptional
reverence. A group of kneeling angels has lifted the
naked Christ Child from the ground and is offering
him up, one of them devoutly touching his foot, to the
prayerful adoration of the Virgin Mary. The space left
in the foreground encourages the devotee, like the
young St. John, to imaginatively enter their enchanted
circle. The motif of assisting angels is more common
to northern European painting and the gesture of
holding up the child is very rare at this date.[4] Implied
here is a double devotion: firstly to the Virgin Mary as
humble mother of God but also to the body of Christ.
The mystery of God made flesh is also strongly
enhanced by the fact that the Child has left his trace
on the ground where his body was lying, in the form
of a sunburst with a foreshortened face. This mark of
grace clearly mirrors the three bursts of light in the
sky that issue from a series of winged, cherubic
heads. What would once have been the most
dazzling of these, with tongues of flame, appears
above John the Baptist. As well as being the patron

Fra Filippo Lippi (1406 (?) – 1469)
*Adoration of the Child with St. Bernard and John the
Baptist,* c. 1459, 129.5 x 118.5 cm,
Staatliche Museen zu Berlin, Gemäldegalerie

[1] The motto and its
owner are referred to by
Popham and Pouncey,
1950, I, *Addenda*, p.
209.

[2] Degenhart and
Schmitt (1968, p. 557)
point convincingly to
the model of the lost
central panel of a small
triptych Lippi was
making for the King of
Naples in 1457. A small
sketch at the bottom of
Lippi's letter to
Giovanni de' Medici,
who had commissioned
the altarpiece, shows us
the Virgin adoring the
Christ Child who is
surrounded by kneeling
angels (also reproduced
by Degenhart and
Schmitt, cat. no. 359
and fig. 302b).

[3] Reproduced in colour
in R. Bacou, *Drawings in
the Louvre: The Italian
Drawings*, London 1968,
no. 5 (not paginated).
Popham and Pouncey
connected our drawing
to the workshop of
Andrea del Verrocchio
and dated it to c. 1470.

[4] One example (Kress
Collection no. 1856,
present location
unidentified) is that by
an Austrian master of c.
1480.

DOMEN.^{co} GHIRLAN=
=DAIO.

25

saint of Florence, John was the first to acknowledge Christ in his ministry and thus appears as a young witness to the Lamb of God in Filippo Lippi's Medici palace altarpiece (illustrated p. 24). A trio of shining heads appears at the centre of the sky, while the weakest apparition, to the right, is aligned with the marginalized Joseph. These, then, are not guiding stars of the Nativity but, like the shell-gold spiral rays used in Lippi's painting, represent the emanations of heavenly grace associated with the Incarnation. The fanciful but orchestrated landscape setting, with its rhythmic row of shielding hills, decorative Tuscan trees and dotted settlements is illuminated from the left and, with the darkening of the vellum, has lost much of its original luminescence. The drawing as a whole, however, has maintained its poised charm. The all-important drapery patterns of the kneeling figures, with tubular folds decoratively pooling onto the ground, have been precisely outlined in pen before being brought to life by controlled use of wash (the brush dipped in diluted ink). The quality of the drawing is particularly apparent in the heads, especially that of the demure Virgin and the four young angels with foreshortened haloes. While one turns back to Christ with eyes downcast, the angel nearest to the

beholder looks up to the Virgin in a gesture of appeal, completing a circuit of adoring gazes that includes the baby's own. This is an intimately domestic treatment of the Nativity, typical of the middle decades of the fifteenth century, in which the mediation of the angels and saints is designed to encourage the devotion of lay (secular) viewers. It closely compliments the production and consumption of empathetic, sometimes mystical, devotional literature of a kind especially directed towards women and children: just those groups who would find role models in this picture.

5. Head of a Child

British Museum 1946,0713.1260
Pen and brown ink on paper, extensively rubbed,
stuck down.
14.9 x 12.6 cm (irregular),
Inscribed on mount: "And[rea]. Mantegna."

Select bibliography: Popham, 1935, p. 2, no. 1.

Drawn slightly under life size, and now closely cropped around the head, this fragile sheet offers an intriguingly immediate encounter. In cat. no. 4 we have seen the recumbent baby held up for adoration; here we are led to admire, rather, the difficult angle of the foreshortened head of a real child and to wonder at its status. He or she appears to be wearing swaddling bands but has a toddler's head of hair. Is it sleeping, or lifeless, as such a recumbent subject seen radically from below so often is in Italian Renaissance images? The likelihood that this drawing was made with some well-known pictorial task in mind - the Virgin adoring the sleeping Christ Child or even the Massacre of the Innocents – would not fully resolve this tension. While the 'sitter' is surely a living, sleeping child, it offers a model adaptable both to death and that disturbing sleep that prefigures death encountered, for example, in Giovanni Bellini's great *Madonna of the Meadow* (National Gallery, London, c. 1500). The artist has used a flexible pen system that utilizes a net of hatchings and cross-hatchings to build up shadow and describe the form. Thus the curving lines around the tip of the nose or down the near cheek produce an impression of salient features emerging from an almost smoky half-darkness. Light appears to fall from above the forehead but there is also a prominent reflected light under the chin. In all, the effect is powerfully volumetric, almost sculptural, and seems to be the product of intense looking. Such scrutiny is, not surprisingly, rare in relation to a subject that is normally so unaccommodatingly mobile. This sense of stillness draws the viewer to trace the gentle curves of the yet undefined facial landscape and, while such a viewpoint looking up the nose is potentially ugly, the effect here is highly contemplative and delicate. As an ambitiously worked up head study the drawing is close in type and function to that of the head of a 'dead' youth drawn by Pisanello around 1430, now in the Louvre. The ascription on the mount of our drawing to Andrea Mantegna responds rather to the later northern Italian master's famous skill in foreshortening (compare the child in his early *Adoration of the Shepherds* panel from the San Zeno altarpiece or the *Dead Christ* in Milan). Mantegna, too, was able to produce sculptural effects in his drawings by using parallel hatching, but these skills were well disseminated in north-eastern Italy and the Marches by the 1460s so this does not locate the origin of this drawing very closely. Despite its luminous directness, the drawing comes to us through a veil of age, with the pen work heavily rubbed and the paper stained. If anything, this only adds to the pathos of our encounter with this nameless and vulnerable child. Oblivious to the gaze of the draughtsman, and now to our own, it seems to sleep in the shadow of mortality. Whatever age the subject may have survived to, the visible age of the drawing only affirms the ancient adage 'art is long and life short'.

1670   And. Mantegna.

6. Man in a long mantle seen from behind

British Museum 1952,0121.83
Metalpoint and white heightening on cream prepared paper. Stuck down.
21.4 cm x 9.6 cm (area of original paper 19.7 cm high)

Select bibliography: Pouncey and Gere, 1962, cat. no. 81 (for the Cavendish Album of drawings, of which the present sheet formed part from the early eighteenth century. Probably collected by James Cavendish, son of the second Duke of Devonshire).

Whereas in catalogue no. 2 the onlookers remain nameless because we are not given enough information to identify them as saints, the bystander preserved in this much later drawing has a different anonymity. Shown in 'lost profile' facing away from the viewer, he is at once an example of a type and tantalizingly related to a real individual, albeit one whose name we will never know. Based on observation of a live model it apparently belongs to a common Renaissance type, the so-called *garzone* study in which a member of the painter's workshop is shown posed in appropriate costume. It may have been made in preparation for a particular commission but such drawings, produced in large numbers usually in metalpoint or pen and ink, were more often than not intended to train the draughtsman's hand and eye and to supply a figure type that could be used across a whole range of painting or design tasks. The identity of the person observed was quite unimportant and the figure might gain different, and more specific, features at the painting stage. In the present example we are shown a figure modelling the type of the dignified young patrician. He wears a variant of civic dress and a close fitting cap over the luxuriant locks typical of the last decades of the fifteenth century in Florence. What distinguishes the type as a man of worldly means is above all his slightly swaggering, off-centre pose, a pose that produces a wealth of drapery effects visible from behind. With the weight planted on his foreshortened right foot and left foot extended, his head emerges above a great column of drapery marking the central axis of his elongated and concealed body. Around the swathed left arm the heavy mantle breaks forward or dives into shadow, forming a contrived fold pattern that contrasts to the stable right side. The effect is not only formally decorative but highly functional, providing a graceful *repoussoir*, or figure of closure, to the right hand side of a larger composition. The profile of the face could also lead the viewer back towards the centre of a religious story, drawing them in as a kind of co-witness. Good examples of this handy figure type in action include the bystanders in Domenico Ghirlandaio's frescoed narratives of the 1480s and 1490s – a close relative of our figure appears to the right of St. Francis Renouncing his Worldly Goods in the Florentine Sassetti Chapel, completed in 1485.[1] In the British Museum drawing, the contained boldness of the pose is offset by the understatement of the technique. Like a number of later fifteenth-century Florentine painters, the draughtsman has reverted to the use of metalpoint (used much earlier in cat. no. 1) for figure and drapery study. A stylus, probably of lead in this case, provides a delicate but indelible line when used on roughened prepared paper, and, drawn over the surface in controlled parallel hatching strokes, it can produce subtle effects of relief. To extend the poor tonal range of the stylus, the artist has applied white lead pigment with a brush along the drapery and profile on the side nearest the light and added further hatching beyond to make the left arm stand out further. His efforts are now compromised by the oxidization of the lead white, which - following the same chemical process that allows the stylus line to become visible in the first place - has turned black.

[1] For a figure drawing of the same pose and effect see C.L. Ragghianti and G. Dalli Regoli, *Firenze 1470-1480. Disegni dal modello*, Pisa 1975, cat. 153 (on the reverse of a drawing by the Florentine painter Fra Bartolommeo); for a drawing of this type in the same technique see L. Melli. *I disegni italiani del Quattrocento nel Kupferstich-Kabinett di Dresda*, Florence 2006, cat. no. 32, pp. 164-7.

31

7. Two naked youths fighting

British Museum 1854,0628.59, Popham and Pouncey cat. no. 310
Pen and brown ink over black chalk on white paper
23.8cm x 26.9 cm

Select Bibliography: Waagen, 1854, I, p. 224; Waagen, 1857, p. 30; Popham and Pouncey, 1950, I, p. 194; Kristeller, 1901, p. 461.

The naked male figure began to be re-valued as a fundamental artistic challenge already by the third decade of the fifteenth century. By the later fifteenth century, when the present drawing was made, the vigorous male body had become a favourite subject for the display of artistic invention in draughtsmanship, demonstrating anatomical expertise and, importantly, knowledge of admired antique sculptures. As this ambitious sheet shows, the naked figure in combat was also a subject through which a range of conceptions about ideal male conduct could be presented. One of the most famous early essays in the genre took the form of an engraving, signed by Antonio del Pollaiuolo, showing a battle of nude warriors whose vicious engagement - in tight groups or pairs using a variety of hand weapons - takes place in an unspecified, and apparently uncivilized, past. Our sheet owes something to this model, as well as to other northern Italian drawings in which naked soldiers appear in groups simultaneously putting the affective male body through its paces and the abilities of the draughtsman on display (see illustration, also from the British Museum). A particular feature of this graphic virtuosity is the tendency to counterpose figures in complimentary pairs so that, through viewing a figure seen from the front against one from behind, the viewer is encouraged to imagine the corporeal unity of a fully three-dimensional figure occupying space. In the present pairing the draughtsman also sets off the slightly enlarged heads against one another – one seen ambitiously turned in three-quarter view from below, the other in 'lost' profile. First laying down the poses using a black chalk underdrawing (especially visible where the naval has been shifted), the draughtsman has produced a subtle effect of relief and bodily softness using an extremely refined system of parallel hatching in pen. The same technique highlights how limbs project or recede in space. Once attributed to the Florentine Pollaiuolo and later connected, more plausibly, with the style of the Paduan painter Mantegna who knew Pollaiuolo's designs, our drawing reveals a quite different sensibility from either of these masters.[1] Despite following the Florentine model of muscularity and dynamism, emphasizing contours (rather too evenly here) and lining up limbs, the effect in this drawing is curiously slow-moving, balletic and without conviction as combat. What might have been a gesture of aggressive intervention by the left hand figure, to be swiftly followed up by the brandished sword, has become something more like an embrace. Similarly the club-wielder, while prepared to retaliate with his erect yet unthreatening club, seems keener to lock gazes than weapons. It is above all the characterization of these curly haired youths and the heavily sensuous, idealised, almost dreamy features of the former, so unlike Pollaiuolo's contorted physiognomies, that suggest the instant of mutual admiration. Offered a full frontal view of their complementary nudity the viewer is drawn in as an observer of, but also a third party to, the implicit eroticism of the encounter. Heroic or barbaric, antique or timeless, aggressive or sensual, the allure of the drawing lies in the way it holds together these contradictory appraisals. Regardless of whether - or how - the viewer relishes the men's actions and the classicising model of male beauty they propose, such finished penmanship, achieving effects both fleshy and analytical, was meant to encourage the admiring gaze.

Antonio del Pollaiuolo, *A prisoner led before a ruler, pen and brown ink and wash on paper,* 36.9 x 69.3 cm, ©*The Trustees of the British Museum* 1893-5-29-1

[1] Attributed in the Woodburn sale catalogue to Andrea Mantegna and then in the Museum register as Pollaiuolo, it was regarded by Paul Kristeller as near to Pollaiuolo 'but it seems to us to be Paduan'. In fact a number of Paduan artists knew Pollaiuolo's graphic work on the subject the male nude, not least because a large sheet existed in the prominent collection of the painter Francesco Squarcione.

33

8. St. Sebastian
Verso: Black chalk head of a man in profile with eyes closed

British Museum 1895,0915.800, Popham and Pouncey cat. no. 18
Pen and brown ink with wash and white heightening on pink prepared paper.
18.6 x 5.8cm

Select bibliography: von Hadeln, 1925, plate 54 and pp. 38 and 48; Tietze and Tietze-Conrat, 1944, no. 308, pp. 86-7; Popham and Pouncey, 1950, I, p. 12; Robertson, 1968, p. 42; Goldner, 2004, p. 236.

The emotional impact of this compelling drawing rests on a tension between the composure of the male body beautiful and the signs of a suffering soul, made eloquent in the saint's searching, hollow-eyed expression. Despite the shift from pagan to Christian subject matter, the concerns of the drawing are closely related to those of cat. no. 7 depicting battling nudes. Here, again, is the interest in classicising proportions and the description of the body in terms of muscular articulation, emphatic contour and the directional fall of light. And, while here the figure is more decorously draped with a loincloth, the exposure of the hip lip where the cloth has slipped to the top of the thighs, gives the youthful figure a contained sexual charge. This is not at all untypical for the depiction of St. Sebastian in Venice or Florence in the later decades of the fifteenth century – indeed a much racier version of the subject by the engraver Jacopo de' Barbari around 1500 testifies to this appeal. The effect of our drawing is, nonetheless, quite different to that of cat. no. 7, not least because of the statuesque character of the saint. His pose relates to Graeco-Roman models of a 'contrapposto' pose found in ancient reliefs and also freestanding sculpture, where a long vertical profile (here to the right, reinforced with dark ink) is contrasted to that of the supporting leg. Distinct, too, is the treatment of the medium. Rather than using an orderly graphic system with a quill, the ink – in two colours and at least three different tones - has been applied with a brush alone. Across the skin, the tip of the brush has been plied in short vertical strokes to produce a warmly atmospheric and painterly effect that is strongly enhanced by the choice of a pinkish ground. Complementing the 'sculptural' body, the saint is bound, none too emphatically, to a half-buried classical pier or pilaster strewn around with stones. This would have reminded the viewer – as it does in Andrea Mantegna's contemporary essays in the isolated St. Sebastian – of the era of the soldier's martyrdom under the Emperor Diocletian. The ruin of this old world order is anticipated in the crumbling architectural features dimly visible behind him. St. Sebastian's body is displayed, then, as a Christ-like body that suffers persecution in order to forward Christianity's triumph over paganism. For contemporaries, however, his body also played a more immediate role, which gave his image a further poignancy and a potency that transcended the exemplary. It was believed that by praying to the saint the devotee would be spared the 'arrows' of the plague: Sebastian's intercession with God for the faithful would absorb or deflect disease, just as his body had absorbed the arrows of persecution. It is in this guise that the intercessory saint appeared with great frequency in altarpieces and other panels of the period. In our drawing not only does the saint appear alone, as is typical for 'devotional' versions of the martyred saint, but without the arrows of martyrdom, allowing the viewer to appreciate the smooth planes of the broad-shouldered and unblemished body. It is likely that arrows would have been added only at the painting stage, and, even then, only peripherally in order to downplay the evidence of physical torture more common to earlier representations of the saint. In this otherwise complete preparatory study the pain is firmly located in the psyche: in the pathetic head of the saint and in the mind of the sympathetic viewer. Sebastian looks up to heaven but also into the darkness with an open-mouthed cry of anguish and, following his gaze, the viewer imaginatively anticipates both his suffering and heavenly reward. Sebastian's body is transfigured by light but it is not transfixed. The horror is therefore displaced imaginatively so that the devotee who knows the saint's story may see, or project, a kind of shudder running through the drapery of the saint's closely described loincloth.

This captivating drawing is an interloper in the present exhibition in as much as the tentative category 'attributed to Giovanni Bellini' alloted to it in 1950 Italian drawings catalogue of the British Museum is probably over cautious. The beauty and assurance of the sheet, even in its present state, is such that for several art historians, including this writer, the balance tips in favour of it as an autograph work. Close in feeling to Bellini's *Blood of the Redeemer* panel (National Gallery, London) it seems to have been made at a moment in the 1460s when the great Venetian painter was learning from the work of Andrea Mantegna though already offering a new colouristic and devotional sensibility. In this sheet, drawing too is reconfigured with reference to a distinctly Venetian poetics of painting.

9. Three heads

British Museum 1907,0717.31, Popham and
Pouncey cat. no.14
Black chalk on cream paper, stuck down.
13 x 19.8 cm to edge of original sheet

Select bibliography: Popham and Pouncey, 1950, I,
p. 9; Scharf, 1952, p. 210; Robertson, 1968, p. 133;
Turner, 1994, no. 21; Goldner, 2004, p. 254.

The original appeal of this drawing probably lay in the way it matches a series of 'ancient' and exotic types, which look like Roman sculpted heads, with a painterly immediacy of treatment. This immediacy follows from black chalk's capacity to imitate the texture of skin as well as from the draughtsman's interest in evoking the inner life of his subjects. While the central figure has highly individualized features, which suggest a contemporary model, he is wearing a form of ancient toga and the suppression of background makes the temporal setting of the group deliberately generalized. Such an ambiguity – is this present, ancient or 'timeless'? - allows for an allegorical or moralized reading of the drawing, explored further below. The draughtsman appears to have taken the central man first, since he alone has any bodily presence. The turbaned figure (now cropped) and the youthful, androgynous beauty to the right - presumably a woman with ornamentally dressed hair in an antique fashion - are added to frame him. The viewer's eye passes from one figure to another and reads them relationally so that, taken together, they suggest not only a variety of types and sexes but, strikingly, a juxtaposition of ages. The tallest figure at the centre, seen fractionally from below, becomes a figure of experienced old age whose penetrating gaze, beneath beetling brows, is directed upwards and beyond into the light, as though to some future goal. While his mind may be turning from worldly concerns, his worn features testify to a past life marked by adversity. In particular we are invited to read in the heavily distorted (badly broken?) nose and scarred ear, the type of the old warrior, a subject beloved of earlier artists like Verrocchio and Leonardo da Vinci. Here, though, the warrior has turned philosopher and looks for insight, apparently towards the next life. To the left is a man in middle life whose pale gaze is even and controlled, giving little away. To the right, the viewer's own gaze is brought to rest on the full, passive face of youth. With straying locks framing her face, she looks down with lips slightly parted in an expression that is both earth-bound and self-absorbed, the antithesis of the active transcendence implied by the old man. Seen in these terms, we may be looking at a platonic meditation in which the body - however its beauty may point to a lost ideal - is only ever a prison for the mind. The philosopher looks for a lost heavenly perfection and the hope that his immortal soul will find release from the body after death. Less specifically, and more certainly, we are presented with the topic of the Ages of Man. This theme, which was common only to Venice, evokes meditation on different ages of life (usually three): youth or adolescence, maturity and old age. The painter Titian treated the theme in pastoral form in his landscape with a shepherd, a hermit saint and sleeping children now in Edinburgh (National Gallery of Scotland). The Venetian painting known as the *Concert or Singing Lesson* in the Galleria Palatina, Florence, with half-length figures against a dark ground, has also been interpreted in this light. Closest to our drawing in its elegiac mood, if not in formal terms, is Giorgione's *Three Philosophers* in Vienna, which also characterizes the middle-aged figure as Eastern. In each case, art historical debates about the 'true' subject of these paintings are a reminder that Venetian inventions of the early decades of the sixteenth century, like our drawing, often worked on a deliberately open and contemplative register. This allowed viewers the intellectual pleasure of finding parallel and multiple readings as well as the emotional satisfaction of indulging wistful sympathy. One major pleasure afforded by the British Museum drawing lies in tracing the work of the chalk itself in the hands of a 'painterly' draughtsman. When following the rugged landscape of old age, the chalk is sharpened to describe the tough folds of skin over a bone structure rendered ever more visible by time. By contrast, the flawless, swelling softness of the plump features of the girl are achieved by rubbing the parallel strokes of the chalk laid over the cheeks and chin line. What emerges, in the strongly directional light is a revelation both of mood and of physiognomy. This encourages the beholder to linger and give the drawing the attention normally reserved to a painting. Indeed this sheet may well have been made as a graphic challenge on its own terms, rather than as preparatory to a specific painting. It is stylistically close to Giovanni Bellini and could, in this case, be by a member of his talented workshop, anthologizing some of his new figure types.

10. Portrait drawing of a man

British Museum inv. no. 5218-47, Popham and
Pouncey cat. no. 330
Black chalk on pale brown (darkened?) paper.
39.9 x 31.5 cm

Select bibliogaphy: Colvin, 1908/9, 8; Tietze and
Tietze-Conrat, 1944, no. 802, p. 190; Popham and
Pouncey, 1950, I, p. 199; Agosti, 2001, p. 155; Greer
in *Renaissance Faces*, 2008, no. 81, pp. 252-3

This compelling drawing of a man, shown life-size, has
an intriguing double anonymity, since we know
neither the artist nor its subject. The relative
suppression of style contingent on producing a
likeness is intrinsic to the genre of the portrait, a genre
that became independent of religious contexts in the
Renaissance. Nonetheless, the impulse to identify has
proved strong when confronted with such an
obviously individualized set of features as those of the
British Museum drawing. Despite the fact that both
the bust- length portrait type and the choice of
technique - black chalk – are common in late
fifteenth- and early sixteenth-century Venice, an early
commentator was keen to recognize the work of the
great German painter Albrecht Dürer. The ambiguous
identification 'bust of man resembling A. Dürer'
(1837) later became an identification of him as the
sitter, sporting a neatly trimmed 'German' beard, but
drawn by another, Venetian hand, during Dürer's
second stay in Venice (Colvin, 1908/9). But, whether
a self-portrait or not, the naming of Dürer was
certainly wishful thinking. His well-known features
are quite different and as a foreigner he is unlikely to
have been allowed to adopt the costume of a Venetian
citizen. Our sitter, as Elena Greer recently reaffirmed,
wears a type of dark gown, cap and a stole (here rather
narrow, like a university doctor's stole, and tucked into
the official 'toga') that mark him out as either a citizen,
or patrician gentleman, in the Venetian Republic.[1] It
is this public role that dominates the identity
communicated by the portrait. The remarkably even
hatching of the gown, now truncated, serves as a rigid,
immutable and dignified support for the carefully
groomed head. Giving a sense of elevation, the viewer
appears to look up slightly at the mouth while
meeting the steady gaze straight on. The framing curls
and distinctively trimmed beard further stabilize the
features while showing off the draughtsman's skill at
coaxing textural effects from the black chalk. Parallel
curling strokes describe locks of dark hair that are
played off against the clear planes of taut flesh.
Around the all-important eye area, creases of skin and
nuances of light are described with minuteness,
though the liquid eyes themselves convey little about
the personality. Thus the control of the drawing
technique seems well matched to the highly
controlled attitude of this sitter, who perhaps chose to
be recorded in the prime of his active life. Unlike
Antonello da Messina's or Andrea Mantegna's strongly
characterized male portrait sitters, the subject looks
guarded and uncommunicative, with all suggestion of
movement confined to the hairs that escape from
under the cap or fringe out around the head. Yet the
effect of a moment caught, as against a permanent
state, is subtly suggested by the direct gaze and by the
rather low and specific fall of light that allows the end
of the cap band to cast a shadow. Time will pass and
the shadow will move. Given its state of finish, the
sheet was almost certainly made as a completed work
in its own right, like a number of other portrait
drawings in chalk that survive by Mantegna and
northern Italian contemporaries produced in the years
around 1500. Like catalogue no. 9, showing three
heads in the same medium, its closest relation is to
painting. Indeed the portrait's large scale, and the
practiced handling of a dark chalk offer a sense of
immediacy and atmospheric glow that is the absolute
graphic equivalent of Venetian oil painting at its most
refined. Though the drawing lacks colour and, with it,
the social signaling available to coloured cloth, the
advantages to the sitter of a likeness on paper were
many: speed of execution, portability and, relative to a
painting, its minimal cost.

[1] For this costume, its variants and its regulation see S.M Newton. *The Dress of the Venetians, 1495-1525*, Aldershot and Vermont 1988, pp. 9-23.

39

11. Chalice design

British Museum1893,0731.20, Popham and
Pouncey cat. no. 327
Pen and brown ink on vellum.
48.4 x 26.5 cm

Select bibliography: British Museum, *Guide*, 1895,
no. 46; Hind, 1910, no. 29 at pp. 292-3; Popham
and Pouncey, 1950, I, no. 327, p. 197; Penny in
Patronage and Collectin, p. 46, cat. no. 50; Agosti,
2004, p. 148.

The piece of goldsmith work represented in this
magnificent drawing is a chalice for holding the wine
in the Christian sacrament of Holy Communion.
Since, in the Catholic rite, the remembrance of the
sacrifice of Christ is believed to entail the
transubstantiation of the bread (in the form of a
wafer) and wine into the actual body and blood of
Christ, the chalice is no mere vessel but a sacred
object. As such, it is considered worthy of the richest
and most honourable design: certainly the present
example would have been suitable for the high altar of
a great church. The broad, Gothic style base has an
impressive number of ogival facets and three steps
raised on pierced designs. The basket weave motif of
the central step recurs on the vase form below the
large, central knop. Supported on horns of plenty, this
traditional element is shaped in an up-to-date way to
resemble a renaissance temple or octagonal tabernacle
with niches for freestanding figures. Finally, a ring of
putti in relief elevate the cup that, unusually, has two
fields of decoration, with late Gothic foliate ornament
below and a figured frieze in an antique style above.
The drawing offers not only ornament but a
theological programme; figures inscribed or cast on
the various levels of the chalice describe a history of
salvation moving upwards from the base. Old
Testament prophets holding scrolls adorn the lowest
zone, Apostles of Christ inhabit the temple and the
cup itself culminates with six low relief (or *nielloed*)
scenes of the Passion of Christ, beginning with what
may be the Raising of Lazarus at the left to the
Flagellation at the right. These scenes can be imagined
continuing on the far side to include the Crucifixion
itself and ultimately the Resurrection. Despite its
slightly over life-size scale, then, the drawing presents a
highly plausible object. In reality, we do not know
whether the chalice ever existed as a usable vessel
either before or after this drawing was made. It is
conceivable that the design was intended to record a
particularly exquisite and costly work or that it was
produced in the hope of persuading a wealthy patron
to have one made. That it served as some kind of
presentation drawing is further suggested by the
support - a carefully scraped and smoothed vellum,
folded once down the middle to establish the central
axis of the design. Certainly the drawing was intended
to last and it has enjoyed a long history of admiration.
It was treasured at an early date in the great collection
of the Earl of Arundel, where it was thought to be by
Andrea Mantegna, and was later owned by the painter
Sir Thomas Lawrence. An engraved copy by
Wenceslaus Hollar (1640) was made while the
drawing was in Arundel's collection and a far cruder
engraving (Hind, 1910, no. 29) was subsequently
produced, probably at a much later date. Sidney
Colvin who, at the turn of the last century, was the
drawing's keeper in the British Museum, thought that
it may have been made by a goldsmith from Murano,
near Venice, where much beautiful plate was produced
by the late fifteenth century. Although many drawings
for goldsmith work survive by big name
painter/designers such as Andrea Mantegna, Albrecht
Dürer or Hans Holbein, Renaissance goldsmiths,
most of whose works are now nameless, also had a
reputation for graphic skill.[1] It seems likely that the
combined minuteness of finish and large scale of this
drawing testify to the extraordinary patience and hand
control that was as much a prerequisite of engraving
or casting designs on metal as of graphic art on paper.
The meticulously regular hatching to produce a sense
of relief, the foreshortening of figures on the base and
the use of an overall perspective to position the viewer
(the eye-level is just below the temple) also give the
object a sense of real presence. When referring to the
Real Presence of Christ however, such devices are,
tellingly, abandoned; the half circle of the wafer in the
cup is totally abstracted, as though beyond
representation. The fact that the drawing refers not
just to the blood but to the Body of Christ may also
point to a secondary devotional function,
anticipating seventeenth-century prints that include
the eucharistic chalice. The band of narrative
ornament reminds the viewer of the last days and
death of Christ and the inclusion of a chalice-within-
the chalice *(a mise-en-abyme)* in the tiny scene of the
Agony in the Garden alludes to the chalice's symbolic
role in salvation. Christ is shown praying that the
figurative 'cup' of his sacrificial death might pass
from him, before then submitting to God's will. Seen

[1] Comparable in
decorative vocabulary,
composition and figure
style are a set of five,
equally meticulous,
relief plaquettes with
scenes of the Passion
drawn in pen and ink in
a Mantegnesque graphic
idiom, now in the
Albertiana, Vienna, inv.
nos. 13129-13133.

41

in this devotional light, the almost obsessive completeness of the drawing – its focus on the descriptive and explanatory work of drawing, rather than its inventive or inspirational role - takes on a new significance. What is clearly a patient work of artisanal labour becomes the anonymous draughtsman's labour of love. As viewers, we are encouraged to value and evaluate the work through attentive looking. But the act of drawing implicitly also has a heavenly audience here, one that receives the artist's time and skill as a kind of sacrifice, not fully explained within the terms of trade and civic recognition.

43

12. St. John the Evangelist, after Jacopo Sansovino

National Gallery of Scotland, Edinburgh D. 1896
Red chalk and red wash over traces of black chalk on buff paper, squared in black chalk.
26.3 x 12.2 cm

Select bibliography: Andrews,1968, p. 150; Scrase in *Genius of Venice*, cat no. D52, p. 279; Boucher, 1991, I, pp. 65-7, II, pp. 331-2, p. 378, cat. no. 133; Weston-Lewis in *Age of Titian*, cat. no. 94, pp. 232-3

This sheet records the process of a draughtsman looking both backwards in time at an earlier model and forwards to a future task. The artist's existing model is a sculpted high relief figure of St. John the Evangelist by the Florentine Jacopo Sansovino designed, at about 30 cm tall, for the bronze doors of the sacristy of St. Mark's in Venice. The future task requires the squaring of the drawing, using a black chalk grid, for expansion to a more monumental scale. In looking back, the artist absorbed still earlier sculpted models: the boldly turned head and heroic features of the saint are dependent on antique statuary. Sansovino himself seems also to have had in mind two Florentine monumental sculptures in marble, Donatello's early Renaissance statue of St. Mark with its naturalistic drapery articulating an antique 'contrapposto' pose and Michelangelo's commanding, but unfinished, St. Matthew. The advantages to a painter of a sculpted model rather than a live one are obvious, allowing time for exploration of the three-dimensionality of a difficult pose without tiring a workshop model who may also have lacked the right physique. Here, the draughtsman seems to have begun at the head using black chalk to describe the curls of hair and mark the ear (now visible on the near cheek) before moving the whole head further to the left and changing to red chalk. Perhaps he did this in order to achieve a warmer lighting effect; certainly this would have been an unusual choice of medium if he was a Venetian draughtsman. Using now a very dark red, rather friable, chalk he first described the contours of the figure and drapery and then turned to parallel hatching the areas of shadow down the right side of the body and across the background, forming a surface against which the figure could project in relief. Taking up the brush he then applied two kinds of red wash. One is used to strengthen or correct the dark accents all round the figure, including the shadows cast by the feet, and to raise the line of the hem (to our left) so that it produces a continuous curve. The second, lighter, wash reinforces the paler shadows and softens the background. The dark area to the right looks at first like a stain but must represent a deeper shadow since it purposefully avoids the projecting book. In this richly worked study, then, the draughtsman seems not to be simply observing but adjusting and correcting a model. In fact he has omitted the book upon which Sansovino's saint rests his bent leg and removed the further reaches of the mantle so that it no longer falls to the floor behind the figure. While the saint appears to be standing on a ledge and is consistently lit, there is no evidence of the niche that contains the bronze statuette. Taken together with the meticulous execution and softness of finish it seems likely in fact that, as Aidan Weston-Lewis has suggested, the drawing is based on some kind of figure in wax or clay rather than on the bronze itself. The latter, standing slightly above eye-level to the left of the relief of the Resurrection of Christ, would not have been on view before 1572, some two years after Sansovino's death. But the commission for the doors from the Procurators of St. Mark's was made already in 1546 so it is quite possible that a model for St. John could have been available before the '70s. What the drawing studies, and accentuates, is the heroic, monumental gesture of the head, the commanding grasp of the hands and the careful articulation of the balance of the body overlaid with sober folds of drapery, all characteristics of the great Tuscan sculptural tradition from Donatello to Michelangelo. But in the translation to Venice, both Sansovino's sculpture and these weighty precedents are transformed. Caught in a soft flood of light, the model seems to have been conjured back into flesh and blood, ready, perhaps, for a new life in painting.

45

13. Studies of sculpture in S. Agostino, Rome
Verso: Red chalk study of a bent leg and foot

Courtauld Gallery, London, D.1952.RW.2535
Pen and brown ink on greyish paper over some black chalk.
Inscribed top centre: In Roma in Sto Augustino
bottom left: ..o di nel 1581. (in grey ink) da me ritratto
top right: 1581 s(e)tem(bre) 14

17.7. x 18.2 cm

Select bibliography: Bonito,1982 (for the Goritz chapel of St.Anne, the Virgin and Christ); Montevecchi, 1985, pp. 52-58 (Goritz chapel), and pp. 91-92 (chapel of the Virgin).

The various Italian inscriptions on this sheet - in several different inks but apparently by the same hand - indicate it was the product of a late sixteenth-century study visit to a particular Roman church on a particular day: September 14th, 1581. That the draughtsman himself was not a native to the city is suggested by the note 'In Roma' before the location Sant' Agostino. Added at the bottom left of the sheet is the somewhat superfluous statement 'portrayed by me'. We will probably never know who 'me' was, for the drawing is strictly functional in character and subordinates aesthetic effects to the purpose of record. What gives the drawing its personal character is rather the eyewitness aspect of the inscriptions. These both register and order the experiences of the unknown artist, while the drawings themselves clearly show works viewed at first hand, *in situ* rather than in the workshop. The sketches indicate something of the architectural setting and show the draughtsman's particular angle of vision. Drawing with chalk and then quill in a church interior cannot have been very comfortable and it is clear from the economical and sometimes wobbly pen strokes that the artist has tried to grasp the essentials as quickly as possible. Stopping only to change viewpoint and ink between the two studies, he abandons the use of black chalk for underdrawing for the right-hand group, which has been rendered quickly and incompletely. But the record of both subjects, if mechanical, is accurate enough for us to be able to identify them. The left-hand sculpture was famous from its very unveiling some seventy years earlier, in 1512. It is the *Virgin and Child and St. Anne* proudly signed by Andrea Sansovino, master of Jacopo Sansovino whose sculpture is represented in catalogue no. 12. The elder Sansovino's ambitious group was carved to adorn an altar niche on the third nave pier on the left on entering Sant' Agostino (and has now returned there after a sojourn in another chapel) while above it was Raphael's monumental fresco of the seated prophet Isaiah. These complementary works of painting and sculpture had been commissioned in 1510 by the humanist cleric and Apostolic Protonotary, Johann Goritz for what was then intended to be his burial chapel. The subject of the sculpture (discussed further at cat. no. 14), which labelled the triple dedication of the chapel, was an ambitious one and awkward to figure in three-dimensional terms. Andrea Sansovino was trained in Tuscany and his solution to the group, which is both Florentine in its feel for the body revealed under gracefully drapery, and Roman in its characterization of the Virgin, was seen as exemplary. Contemporary poets praised it as rivalling the sculpture of the ancient Greeks, while Giorgio Vasari (1568) also spoke of the group as 'excellent' amongst modern works. Both sculptures shown are installed relatively high and, as the depiction of the plinths indicate, our draughtsman has looked up at them from slightly below. The study in darker ink to the right also includes the projecting cornice above the niche and notes the scroll of what must have been a shell form behind the head of the Virgin and Child group. This second much less well known sculpture, impressive for its richly decorative treatment of drapery, was latterly transferred into the vestibule of the side entrance to Sant' Agostino and is now placed there above a tomb. An earlier written account suggests, however, that it originally adorned an altar placed against a pier on the south aisle of the church, directly opposite the Goritz chapel, and with a Marian tondo above it.[1] Indeed it seems likely that the latter chapel was designed to complement this slightly earlier, and somewhat unusual, ensemble. Our drawing notes the dominant diagonal sweep of the Virgin's mantle in the sculpture, the distinctive concertina of drapery descending from her right arm and the pattern of v-shaped folds below her hand as she lifts the Christ Child tenderly to her face. Though there is a more highly worked red chalk drawing of a leg on the reverse of the Courtauld drawing, that could relate to Raphael's *Isaiah*, the draughtsman of

[1] G. Celio, *Memorie de' nomi degli artefici delle pitture che sono in alcune chiese, facciate e palazzi di Roma*, Naples 1638, ed. E. Zocca, Milan 1967, pp. 16-17 records it and claims it was made by Paolo Romano.

this side of the sheet purposefully excludes the paintings from his purview. Concentrating on the statuary, he turned from one pilaster to the other across the nave, noting how the left-hand group was lit from the left and the other from the right, and how both were brought into relief from the windows of the façade. The church of Sant'Agostino, which had been built for the Augustinian Order by the wealthy French cardinal D'Estouteville (treasurer to the Pope, 1479 – 1483), was a Renaissance basilica at the centre of the city. It was also a great repository of freestanding marble sculpture of the earlier sixteenth century, including Jacopo Sansovino's *Madonna del Parto*, around which a cult developed. It was probably with these sculptures in mind that our anonymous draughtsman visited the church in 1581. Forming a striking contrast to the richly colouristic and pictorial take on sculpture found in catalogue no. 12, the treatment of what he saw, and the choice of what he looked at, strongly suggests that our artistic tourist was a sculptor himself.

49

14. Virgin and Child and St. Anne

Courtauld Gallery, London, D.1952.RW.1832
Red chalk on cream paper, stuck down.
9.3 x 6 cm

Select bibliography: *Hand-list*, p. 94.

The energy and conviction of this tiny drawing seem only intensified by its small scale and the unresolved state of its figures. Formed rapidly from a welter of red chalk strokes, the slashing lines are tempered by the softness and warmth of the medium. Red chalk was little used before the end of the fifteenth century and, with a few grand exceptions, remained uncommon for sketching purposes, as opposed to more worked up studies like catalogue no. 12. Here the draughtsman has used it to lay down, and extensively adjust, his 'first thoughts' on a composition of seated figures, which he has then cropped with a frame, indicating its use for painting. The idea would then have required further refinement through larger, more complete drawings. The intimate family grouping developed here belongs to a devotional subject made famous for Renaissance Italy by Leonardo da Vinci's groundbreaking treatments, such as the 'Burlington House' cartoon, now hung like a painting in the National Gallery, London. The dominant figure to the right is St. Anne, whom legend described as the Virgin's mother. She is seated close to her daughter and reaches across to fondle the chin of the Christ Child as he straddles the Virgin's lap. The Virgin's pose, with its multiple alternatives for the legs, remains unresolved and it is not clear whether it is her left arm that we see reaching towards St. Anne's lap. To the far left, part of a fourth figure has been added in over the Virgin. This is probably St. Joseph, side-lined here by the thematic focus on the maternal lineage of Christ. As in catalogue no. 13, the motif of the Virgin and St. Anne seated side by side may relate to more common northern European Holy Kindred paintings where the Virgin and her mother sit to left and right with the Christ child between them. Leonardo da Vinci's well-known and influential works on the theme, all of them unfinished, show instead the more difficult balancing act in which the younger woman is seated on her mother's lap. Particularly striking for contemporaries was Leonardo's emphasis on the physical and emotional interaction between members of the group so that each seemed to respond to the other. In this way he was also able to introduce a secondary, prophetic theme into the subject that referred to Christ's coming death and the three figures' differing attitudes to it. In the Courtauld Institute sketch, a prophetic dimension is also suggested by the attributes of the Virgin who wears a diadem on her head and supports a book under her right hand. The generous posture of the Christ Child's upper body with the arms spread wide seems also to anticipate, in a suitably understated way, his later gesture of sacrifice on the Cross. Like Leonardo, the draughtsman cleverly draws a further player into the emotional circuit around the Christ Child; in this case the viewer is addressed with disarming directness by Jesus himself. At first glance the child appears to be raising his right hand in blessing too, but a closer look suggests that he might rather be grasping his mother's veil. In reality the gesture is no more complete than many of the other positions of arms, head and legs explored in the sketch. According to Leonardo, rough adjustments, reflecting changes of mind, were not only permissible in the early stage of developing a visual idea but essential if the artist was to avoid resolving arrangements of limbs that did not accord with the 'movements of the mind' of those depicted.[1] Here, for example, the Virgin's head has been shifted to the right, her legs crossed and re-crossed and Christ's proper left leg has been moved back so the foot rests on St. Anne's knee. It is rare for such a slight sketch (*schizzo*) like this one, evidently cut down from a larger sheet, to be preserved. The slightness of a drawing can also make attribution the more difficult and this example has preserved its anonymity even while it retains the direct effect of a distinct hand who was not following a model. One of the few sixteenth-century artists to use red chalk frequently for compositional sketches was the prolific draughtsman Polidoro da Caravaggio (c. 1499 – c. 1543), who worked in Rome from 1515 to1527, mainly on mural projects, before fleeing for Naples and ultimately Messina. He is, incidentally, likely to have been familiar with Andrea Sansovino's sculpture of the Virgin and Child and St. Anne shown in catalogue no. 13. The messy confidence of the chalk lines, the dot or comma accents used for the eyes and the demeanour of the Christ Child are all characteristic for this painter who is also known for his many lively drawings of women and children.[2]

[1] From Leonardo's notes for a treatise on painting (M. Kemp ed. *Leonardo On Painting: An Anthology of Writings by Leonardo da Vinci with a selection of documents relating to his career as an artist*, New Haven and London 1989, p. 222

[2] See for example the small red chalk Virgin and Child study for an Adoration of the Magi in Vienna (Albertina, inv. 362, Sc.R478, Birke and Kertész, 1992-7, I, pp. 203-4) and for a similar handling see the red chalk sketches for the Roman frieze of Caius Marius at Minturno in Amsterdam (Rijksmuseum, Rijksprentenkabinet inv. 1975:91 verso) datable to 1524-5.

51

15. Anamorphic drawing of a rider on a monstrous horse

Courtauld Gallery, London, D.1952.RW.3843
Pen and ink over traces of black chalk on three sheets of paper stuck together.
11.5 cm (left edge), 30 cm, (right edge), 56.7 cm (upper edge), 53.6 cm (lower edge)

Select bibliography: *Hand-list*, p. 95.

The exhibition closes with this large, oddly shaped sheet that purposefully hides its identity. Though the drawing remains unknown to scholars of anamorphic images (from the Greek, 'shaped anew') it belongs to this specialist genre of trick depiction, best known from paintings and prints of the 1530s and 1540s. A famous example is the large anamorphic skull in Hans Holbein's *Ambassadors* double portrait (National Gallery, London), which deliberately disrupts the foreground like an unwelcome smear. The Courtauld sheet is similarly disruptive of the viewer's expectations, being difficult to read when seen straight on. What is instead striking at first glance is the penmanship, employing iron gall ink with a large flexible quill to produce sweeping lines of great variation in tone and width. To the right they describe billows of smoke or cloud and tongues of flame and so encourage the search for clearer signs of representation. What emerges by moving to an oblique angle of vision to the left of the drawing (and, ideally, closing one eye, cf. the digitially manipulated illustration) is a monstrous vision that simultaneously pulls in two directions. A hybrid animal gallops away from the viewer in the same direction as the rapid 'recession' of the paper, with his hooves lost to vision in the clouds, as the image blurs at its further reaches. At the same time a muscular rider, in cloak and helmet, tips back towards the viewer, even as he extends claw-like hands and feet before him. Is he unleashing vengeance or trying to avoid calamity? The gesture, like the message of the sheet, is unclear. More obvious is that, in keeping with the rider's half ancient, half fantastic appearance, his mount is a hybrid: a kind of reverse hippogriff with a horse's head and fiery mane, and a scaly body, which morphs into leonine legs at the rear. The legendary winged hippogriff, whose front half was a griffin and back quarters a horse, was ridden by the sorcerer Atlante and the knight Roger in Ludovico Ariosto's famous epic adventure poem *Orlando Furioso* (published 1516).[1]

But rather than lifting this image directly from the poem, the draughtsman seems deliberately to have forged his own 'furious', almost bestial, invention in order to demonstrate the poetic *fantasia* of the visual artist. The initial disguising of the rider allows the representation, like that of the poet, to unfold over time and produce a metamorphosis that is analogous to the monstrous passage from lion to horse represented in the drawing. The most common subjects for anamorphoses in the Renaissance were actually portraits, including those of rulers whose distinctive features were revealed only when the image was tilted or viewed obliquely under controlled conditions.[2] But printmakers also produced hidden images of foolish or taboo subjects that could be enjoyed for their surprise and entertainment value. It is telling that the earliest anamorphoses reportedly represented horses as well as mythical battles of dragons and lions (Lomazzo, *Trattato della Pittura*, 1584, 335-336). These experimental works were, according to Gian Paolo Lomazzo, made by Leonardo da Vinci in his late years at the court of Francis I in France. Leonardo himself referred to anamorphoses as 'compound' perspectives in which the figure represented was foreshortened (seen from a dramatically oblique angle) as well as the plane on which it was represented.[3] Within the milieu of the French court, such designs as Leonardo's may be understood as an artistic sleight of hand, a witty performance of visual artifice intended to stimulate pleasure and admiration in a limited circle of initiated viewers: those who could discover the secret and enter the game. The appeal of the Leonardesque subject as it is taken up, consciously or not, in this drawing, seems also to rest on the element of surprise. The finding of the 'correct' angle (which is actually 'awry') results in a violent encounter with a terrible horseman, careering at speed into oblivion.[4] The method of construction used here, indicated by the wedge-shaped framing lines, mean that the most effective viewpoint is from the narrow end of the sheet, even though the awkward foreshortening of the rider's muscular leg and the feeble suggestion of wings somewhat undermine the effect. The principal that underpins the anamorphic image, as described in sixteenth- and seventeenth-century sources, was that the lines of sight from the eye to the image - the so-called visual pyramid - had to be projected beyond it onto a plane that was set obliquely behind it, as though the image were casting a shadow. The image, like the shadow of an object hit by low sunlight, will

[1] I am most grateful to Lavinia Harrington for discussing with me, among other things, her ideas on the possible literary 'sources' of the imagery and the best viewing position from which to resolve the image.

[2] Like the 'monstrous' 1546 portrait head of Edward VII now in the National Portrait Gallery that resolved into a portrait only when viewed through a specially provided peep-hole (see the account of Paul Hentzner who saw the portrait in Whitehall in 1598). For the early history of anamorphic images, including the Edward VII, see J. Baltrušaitis, *Anamorphoses: ou, Perspectives curieuses*, Paris 1955, pp. 15 – 36.

[3] M. Kemp, *The Science of Art: Optical themes in western art from Brunelleschi to Seurat*, New Haven and London 1990, at pp. 49-50 and for further on anamorphoses, pp. 208-23;

[4] "Like perspectives, which, rightly gaz'd upon/ Show nothing but confusion; ey'd awry/ Distinguish form'. (Richard II, 2.2 18-20). The reference is noted in Baltrušaitis, 1955, p. 20.

appear broader at the end furthest from the eye. When viewed from the same, oblique point of projection the effect is to re-form the figure. A simple aid to projection was to superimpose a squared grid over the picture or figure that would distort in a regular manner, but there is no trace of the grid method having been adopted here.[5] Instead, the effect is of an impassioned freehand wielding of the pen over a design established in black chalk. Drawing is thus presented as a dynamic activity as rapid and bold as the subject it represents. Once resolved by the viewer's active participation, the drawing offers up its secret. The equestrian image also offers a further, unanticipated, recognition. What presents itself in the penmanship, and the empty, goggle-like eye notations, is a distinctive graphic manner associated with the sixteenth-century Genoese painter Luca Cambiaso. Cambiaso's prolific drawing production included many pen and ink compositions involving frantic horse and rider groups to which the Courtauld sheet can be compared in subject, technique and degree of finish. Primarily active as a fresco painter, so accustomed to working fast, Cambiaso and his efficient workshop treated mythological and Roman history subjects in highly theatrical ways. Many of his Genoese ceiling paintings include both leaping horsemen and strongly foreshortened figures, known as *scorci*, designed to produce an effect of drama when seen from a steep angle from below. Such tasks clearly encouraged Cambiaso's later experiments with designing figures in space according to a graphic method of simplified, cubic forms that were easy to foreshorten. While this interest sits well with the experimental quality of the anamorphic system used here, a system in which the viewer foreshortens the sheet him or herself, the Courtauld drawing is closer stylistically to his earlier draughtsmanship of the later 1550s and 1560s. In particular it recalls Cambiaso's drawings of the Conversion of St. Paul and, another favourite subject, the legendary Roman hero Marcus Curtius who sacrificed himself for his country by driving his horse into the abyss.[6] The painter and theorist Lomazzo commended Cambiaso for his visual 'games', his ability to imagine battles and above all for the '*bizzaria*' or bizarreness of his invented compositions of which many never resulted in paintings. Even though it subsequently fell from grace, such strangeness could be viewed by the mid sixteenth century as a source of pleasure. The '*furia*' of the pen performance and the monstrosity of the drawing is something of an acquired taste, but this taste certainly was acquired by sixteenth-century and seventeenth-century collectors and is further witnessed to on this drawing by the signs of frequent handling. Paradoxically this instantly recognizable and highly 'personal' graphic was, in fact, systematically taught to Cambiaso's many pupils so that they could assist him in his enormous workload. It was also actively adopted, and his drawings freely copied, by Genoese artists who recognized the market value of his idiosyncratic manner. Seen in this context of widespread imitation, what looks like the authorial hand of the master in our drawing is just as likely to be the work of a 'nameless' artist after all.

[5] The method is described by Jean-Francois Niceron (*La Perspective curieuse ou magie artificielle des effets merveilleux*, Paris 1638, pp. 51 ff.)

[6] The comparison with the Hamburg drawing of Marcus Curtius is particularly compelling (E. Schaar, ed. *Italienische Zeichnungen der Renaissance aus dem Kupferstichabinett der Hamburger Kunsthalle*, exh. cat. Hamburg 1997, no. 11, inv. no. 52200); J. Bober, 'I disegni di Luca Cambiaso', in *Luca Cambiaso: Un maestro del Cinquecento europeo*, Milan 2007, pp. 63-83 at p. 71, Fig. 8. Another example is in Christ Church, Oxford (J. Byam Shaw, *Drawings by Old Masters at Christ Church Oxford*, Oxford 1976, cat. no. 1224, I, p. 305, and II, Plate 732). For the Conversion of St. Paul see especially Munich, Staatliche Graphische Sammlung, inv. 2776 and the Florence version in M. Newcome Schleier, *Disegni genovesi dal XVI al XVIII secolo*, exhib. cat. Gabinetto disegni e stampe degli Uffizi, Florence 1989, cat. no. 5, p. 26 there dated to the 1560s.

15. Anamorphic drawing of a rider on a monstrous horse, *(Digitally manipulated to approximate appearance from an oblique view)*

BIBLIOGRAPHY

The Age of Titian: Venetian Renaisance Painting in Scottish Collections, ed.P. Humfrey et al., exhib.cat. National Gallery of Scotland, Edinburgh, 2004.

L.B. Alberti, *On Painting*, transl. (of De Pictura) C. Grayson, ed. Oxford 1991.

G. Agosti, *Disegni del Rinascimento in Valpadano*, Gabinetto disegni e stampe degli Uffizi, Florence 2001.

G. Agosti, 'Su Mantegna, 7 (Nell'Europa del Seicento)', *Prospettiva*, 115-116, 2004, pp. 135-158.

Andrea Mantegna ed. J. Martineau, exhib. cat., Royal Academy of Arts, London, Milan 1992.

K. Andrews, *National Gallery of Scotland: Catalogue of Italian Drawings*, 2 vols., Cambridge 1968.

J. Baltrušaitis, *Anamorphoses: ou, Perspectives curieuses*, Paris 1955.

P. Barocchi and R. Ristori, *Il Carteggio di Michelangelo*, 5 vols. Florence 1965- c. 1983.

B. Berenson, *The Drawings of the Florentine Painters*, amplified edition, 3 vols., Chicago 1938.

V. Birke and J. Kertész, *Die italienischen Zeichnungen der Albertina*, 4 vols.,Vienna 1992-7.

J. Bober, 'I disegni di Luca Cambiaso', in *Luca Cambiaso: Un maestro del Cinquecento europeo*, Milan 2007, pp. 63-83.

V.A. Bonito, 'The St. Anne Altar in Sant'Agostino in Rome: a New Discovery', *Burlington Magazine*, 950, 1982, pp. 269-272.

G. Bora, *I disegni lombardi e genovesi del Cinquecento*, Treviso 1980.

B. Boucher, *The Sculpture of Jacopo Sansovino*, 2 vols., New Haven and London 1991.

British Museum, *Guide to an Exhibition of Drawings and Sketches by Old Masters and by Artists of the English School principally acquired between 1904 and 1912*, London 1912.

British Museum, *Guide to an Exhibition of Drawings and Engravings by the Old Masters principally from the Malcolm Collection in the Print and Drawing Gallery*, London 1895

J. Byam Shaw, *Drawings by Old Masters at Christ Church Oxford*, Oxford 1976.

Catalogue of Drawings exhibited at Messrs. Obach, Nov/Dec 1908.

S. Colvin in *The Academy,* 27, 1884 pp. 338 ff.

S. Colvin in *Gazette des Beaux-Arts*, 30, 1884, p. 282.

S. Colvin in *The Vasari Society for the Reproduction of Drawings by Old Masters*, First Series, 4, 1908/9.

B. Degenhart, *Pisanello*, Turin 1945.

B. Degenhart and A. Schmitt, *Corpus der italienischen Zeichnungen, 1300-1450, Teil I, Süd-und Mittelitalien*, 4 vols. Berlin 1968.

B. Degenhart and A. Schmitt, *Corpus der italienischen Zeichnungen 1300-1450, Teil II, Venedig. Addenda zu Süd- und Mittelitalien,* 3 vols., Berlin 1980.

A. De Marchi, *Gentile da Fabriano*, Milan 1992.

D. Freedberg, 'Why Connoisseurship Matters,' in ed. K. van Stighelen, *Munuscula Discipulorum: Essays in Honour of Hans Vlieghe*, Turnhout 2006, pp. 29-43.

P. Fortini Brown, *Venetian Narrative Painting in the Age of Carpaccio*, Yale 1988.

R. Fry, Editorial, *The Burlington Magazine for Connoisseurs*, 38, no. 218, May 1921, p. 209.

I. Gaskell, 'Drawn by Rembrandt? Reflections on exhibitions and attributions', *Apollo*, 136, 1992, pp. 55-56.

J.A. Gere, 'Some Observations on the Practical Utility of Connoisseurship', in eds. W. Strauss and T. Felker, *Drawings Defined*, New York 1987, pp. 291-305

The Genius of Venice, eds. C. Hope and J. Martineau, exhib. cat., Royal Academy, London 1983.

G. Goldner, 'Bellini's Drawings' in ed. P. Humfrey, *The Cambridge Companion to Giovanni Belllini*, Cambridge 2004, pp. 226-255.

L. Grassi, *Il disegno italiano dal Trecento al Seicento*, Rome 1956.

L. Grassi, *I disegni italiani del Trecento e Quattrocento: scuole fiorentina, senese, marchigiana, umbra*, Venice 1961.

D. von Hadeln, *Venezianische Zeichnungen des Quattrocento*, Berlin 1925.

Hand-list of the Drawings in the Witt Collection, London 1956.

G.F. Hill, *Pisanello*, London 1905.

A.M. Hind, *Catalogue of Italian Engravings in the British Museum*, London 1910, no. 29 at pp. 292-3.

Patronage and Collecting in the Seventeenth Century: Thomas Howard, Earl of Arundel, exhib. cat., Ashmolean Museum, Oxford 1985.

P. Humfrey, 'Pittura e devozione: la tradizione narrativa quattrocentesca' in *La pittura nel Veneto: Il Quattrocento*, I, Milan 1989, pp. 295-342

E. Karet, *The Drawings of Stefano da Verona and his Circle and the Origins of Collecting in Italy: a Catalogue Raisonné*, Philadelphia 2002.

M. Kemp, 'Late Leonardo: Problems and Implications', *Art Journal*, 46, no. 2, 1987, pp. 94-102.

P. Kristeller, *Andrea Mantegna*, London 1901.

G. P. Lomazzo, *Trattato dell'arte della pittura scultura et architettura*, Milan 1584, ed. 3 vols, Rome 1844.

L. Magagnato ed, *Da Altichiero a Pisanello*, exhib. cat. Museo di Castelvecchio, Verona, Venice 1958.

L. Magnani and G. Rossini, *La 'maniera' di Luca Cambiaso: confronti, spazio decorativo, tecniche*, Atti del Convegno, Genova, 2007, Genoa 2008.

R. L. Manning ed., *Drawings of Luca Cambiaso*, exhib. cat. New York 1967, Houston 1974.

R. van Marle, *The Development of the Italian Schools of Painting*, The Hague 1923-1938, especially Vols.VIII, 1927 and XI, 1929.

D. McCarthy, review of the *Nameless* exhibition, *The Burlington Magazine for Connoisseurs*, 38, no. 219, June 1921, pp. 261-2.

L. Melli. *I disegni italiani del Quattrocento nel Kupferstich-Kabinett di Dresda*, Florence 2006.

G.L. Mellini, *Altichiero e Jacopo Avanzi*, Milan 1965.

C.M. Metz, *Imitations of Ancient and Modern Drawings from the Restoration of the Arts in Italy to the Present Time*, London 1798 (expanded edition of 1789).

C. Monbeig Goguel, 'Vasari's Attitude toward Collecting' in P. Jacks, *Vasari's Florence: Artists and Literati at the Medicean Court*, Cambridge 1998, pp.111-136.

B. Montevecchi, *Sant'Agostino, (Le chiese di Roma illustre*, n.s. 17), Rome 1985.

E. Müntz, 'Vittore Pisanello', *Revue de l'art*, 1, 1897, pp. 67-72.

M. Newcome-Schleier, *Disegni genovesi dal XVI al XVIII secolo*, exhib. cat. Gabinetto disegni e stampe degli Uffizi, Florence 1989.

W. Y. Ottley, *The Italian School of Design*, London 1823.

G. Paccagnini, *Pisanello e il ciclo cavallereso di Mantova*, Milan 1973.

Patronage and Collecting in the Seventeenth Century: Thomas Howard, Earl of Arundel, exhib. cat., Ashmolean Museum, Oxford, 1985-6.

T. Pignatti, 'Cinque secoli di pittura nel palazzo dei dogi', *Il palazzo ducale di Venezia*, Florence 1971, pp. 91-217.

Pisanello: Le Peintre aux Sept Vertus, eds. D. Cordellier et al, exh. cat. Musée du Louvre, Paris 1996.

A.E. Popham, *Catalogue of Drawings in the Collection formed by Sir Thomas Phillipps, Bart., F.R.S., now in the possession of his Grandson, T. Fitzroy Phillipps Fenwick of Thirlestaine House, Cheltenham*, I, London 1935.

A.E..Popham, review of Degenhart, *Pisanello*, 1945, in Burlington Magazine, 88, no. 518, 1946, p. 130.

A.E. Popham and P. Pouncey, *Italian Drawings in the Department of Prints and Drawings in the British Museum. The Fourteenth and Fifteenth Centuries*, 2 vols., London 1950.

P. Pouncey and J. Gere, *Italian Drawings in the Department of Prints and Drawings in the British Museum: Raphael and his Circle*, London 1962.

G. Pudelko, 'The Early Works of Paolo Uccello', *Art Bulletin*, 16, no. 3, 1934, pp. 231-259.

G. Pudelko, 'Studien über Domenico Veneziano', *Mitteilungen des Kunsthistorischen Institutes in Florenz* 4, 1934, pp. 144-200.

Renaissance Faces: Van Eyck to Titian, eds. L. Campbell, M. Falomir, J. Fletcher and L. Syson, exhib. cat., National Gallery, London, London 2008.

C.L Ragghianti, *Pittura tra Giotto e Pisanello: Trecento e Quattrocento*, Ferrara 1987.

L. Ragghianti Collobi, *Il Libro de' Disegni del Vasari*, 2 vols. Florence 1974.

J. Richards, *Altichiero: An Artist and his Patrons in the Italian Trecento*, Cambridge 2000.

G. Robertson, *Giovanni Bellini*, Oxford 1968.

A.Scharf, review of Popham and Pouncey, *Burlington Magazine*, 94, 1952, p. 210.

G.Schwartz, 'Connoisseurship: The Penalty of Ahistoricism', *Artibus et Historiae*, 9, no. 18, 1988, pp. 201-206.

S. Skerl Del Conte, 'Pisanello et la culture du XIVe siècle', *Pisanello*, Acts of the Louvre colloquium, June 1996, 2 vols, I, Paris 1998, pp. 45-82.

A. Stix and L. Fröhlich-Bum, *Albertina Katalog, 1, Die Zeichnungen der Venezianischen Schule*, Vienna 1926.

W. Suida in *The Vasari Society for the Reproduction of Drawings by Old Masters*, First series, V, 1909/10, no. 1.

B. Suida Manning and W. Suida eds., *Luca Cambiaso. La vita e le opere*, Milan 1958.

D. Sutton (ed.), 'II. Letters from Herbert Horne to Roger Fry', *Apollo*, 122, July 1985, p. 136.

H. Tietze and E. Tietze-Conrat, *The Drawings of the Venetian Painters in the Fifteenth and Sixteenth Centuries*, New York 1944.

N. Turner, *The Study of Italian Drawings: the Contribution of Phillip Pouncey*, London 1994.

G. Vasari, *Le Vite dei più eccellenti pittori scultori ed architettori*, ed. G. Milanesi, 9 vols., Florence,1878-1885.

G. Waagen, *Treasures of Art in Great Britain*, London 1854.

G. Waagen, *Treasures of Art in Great Britain*, Supplement, London 1857.

F. Wickhoff, 'Über einige italienische Zeichnungen im British Museum', *Jahrbuch der Königlich Preussischen Kunstsammlungen*, 20, 1899, pp. 202-215.

J. Wood, 'Nicholas Lanier (1588-1666) and the Origins of Drawing Collecting in Stuart England' in C. Baker, C. Elam and G. Warwick (eds), *Collecting Prints & Drawings in Europe c. 1500-1750*, Aldershot 2003, pp. 85-121.

W. Wolters, *Der Bilderschmuck des Dogenpalastes*, Wiesbaden 1983.

H. Zerner, 'What gave Connoisseurship its Bad Name?' in eds. W. Strauss and T. Felker, *Drawings Defined*, New York 1987, p. 289-290.